faux florals FOR YOUR WEDDING

Fifty Easy and
Original Projects

CREATIVE
PUBLISHING
international

Chanhassen, Minnesota

Ardith Beveridge, AIFD

faux florals FOR YOUR
WEDDING

Copyright © 2005
Creative Publishing international, Inc.
18705 Lake Drive East
Chanhassen, Minnesota 55317
1-800-328-3895
www.creativepub.com
All rights reserved

CEO: Ken Fund
Vice President/Publisher: Linda Ball
Vice President/Retail Sales: Kevin Haas

FAUX FLORALS FOR YOUR WEDDING

Executive Editor: Alison Brown Cerier
Senior Editor: Linda Neubauer
Managing Editor: Yen Le
Art Director: Rose Woo
Photo Stylist: Joanne Wawra
Production Manager: Helga Thielen
Photographer: Tate Carlson
Photo Direction and Cover Design: Lois Stanfield

Contributors: Bella Creations, Cameo MacGuffin Posy Pockets,
Beverly Colson of Posies in Minneapolis, Design Master,
Galt International, Koehler & Dramm Wholesale Florists,
Mona's Cakes, Schusters of Texas, Smithers-Oasis

Library of Congress Cataloging-in-Publication Data

Beveridge, Ardith.
Faux florals for your wedding :
Fifty easy and original projects / By Ardith Beveridge.
p. cm.
Includes index.
ISBN 1-58923-167-8 (soft cover)
1. Silk flowers. 2. Silk flower arrangement. 3. Weddings. I. Title.
TT890.7.B49 2005
745.92'6--dc22
2004020904

Printed by SNP Leefung Printers Limited:
10 9 8 7 6 5 4 3 2 1

Contents

About the Author

Photo: John S. Maciejny

Ardith Beveridge, AIFD, AAF, PFCI, is a master floral designer, judge, and educator and an expert on wedding designs and trends. She is also the author of *Fabulous Faux Florals*.

Ardith is director of education for the Koehler & Dramm Institute of Floristry. She is the instructor in twelve series of do-it-yourself videos produced by the Floral Communications Group, an endorsed design education specialist for Teleflora wire service, and a master designer for FTD. By special invitation, Ardith has designed for many prestigious events, including presidential inaugurations.

Ardith's enthusiasm and creativity have captivated audiences in programs and workshops across the country and internationally. She has taught both florists and crafters how to create exceptional wedding florals.

Her professional certifications include the American Institute of Floral Designers, American Academy of Floriculture, Professional Floral Communicators International, Society of Floristry LTD (England), and the Canadian Academy of Floral Arts.

Why Faux Florals for Your Wedding?

More and more couples are choosing faux flowers for part or all of their wedding florals. For people who want to create their own wedding flowers, the most important advantage of faux over fresh is that the designs can be created weeks or even months ahead. While a florist can work on your flowers the day before your wedding, you will be just a little busy then!

There are other practical advantages. Faux floral designs are easy to make. The few tools and materials needed are readily available in the wedding and floral departments of craft stores or from neighborhood florists. Transporting faux floral designs to the wedding is easier, too, because the flowers are sturdier, won't wilt or drop petals, and don't need water. Here's a really practical reason to go faux—allergies.

Faux florals also open up many creative possibilities as you plan your wedding. The flowers exist in a huge number of true-to-life styles. You can find exactly the flowers you want, no matter where you live. You will have wider flower choices within your color scheme, too, and some flowers even come in colors that don't exist in nature. Also, you can include flowers that in their natural form would be too fragile for wedding designs.

After the wedding, special pieces like the bouquet become lasting keepsakes (and you won't need to pay to preserve the flowers). You can take other designs apart and use them in table pieces, swags, wreaths, or other decorations for your first home.

Of course, fresh flowers are also wonderful. Actually, you don't have to choose one or the other—it is perfectly acceptable to mix fresh and faux for a wedding. You may want fresh flower bouquets and boutonnieres for the bridal party, for instance, but use faux flowers for reception decorations and favors. You can select as many faux floral projects as you have time to create and leave your fresh flower needs in the hands of a professional florist.

You may want to ask family or friends for help with your faux floral projects. Many brides have a gathering at which bridesmaids or friends make favors and other crafts. A floral craft project is also a special way for a mother or favorite aunt to contribute to the wedding.

I have designed for you more than fifty projects and variations. These designs reflect wedding traditions and trends and my innovations and ideas. Some of the projects may look complicated, but don't worry. The step-by-step photographed instructions assure you professional results, even if you are a beginner.

Ultimately, your wedding is all about your personal style. Florals are a wonderful way to personalize your wedding, and this book will tell you how to do it yourself.

Materials and Techniques

THE FLORALS

Many artificial flowers are so realistic that only a "touch test" detects the difference. In the floral industry, faux florals are properly called "permanent botanicals." Though they are commonly referred to as "silk flowers," most are not made of silk but rather of polyester, latex, parchment, plastic, or a combination of materials.

Faux florals vary widely in quality and price, from inexpensive stems in solid colors to the more expensive realistic stems with shading and veining. Most are made by machine, but some of the more expensive florals are assembled by hand, though the parts may be made by machine. The flowers may be parchment or fabric with wired stems and leaves that are very realistic. Some parchment and fabric flowers are dipped in latex to make them look more natural. "Dried silk" flowers have a crinkled appearance and curled edges that resemble real dried flowers.

Faux florals are produced in four standard forms: bush, fantasy flower, botanical-like, and botanically correct.

Bush. A bush consists of a group of flowers and foliage on one stem, perhaps including accent flowers. Flowers may be of one type or several types. Bushes tend to be reasonably priced and easy to use whole or cut into individual stems.

Fantasy flowers. These flowers resemble real ones but aren't necessarily true to nature. You can find fantasy flowers in all forms and textures to suit your wedding scheme, no matter what colors you choose.

Botanical-like. These florals are closer to the real thing, but the color, stem, foliage, or petal pattern has been changed to suit the desires of consumers. For example, a stem of roses might have baby blue flowers and be free of dying flowers or broken stems.

Botanically correct. These are as close as possible to the real thing— though, of course, without the fragrance. The stem, pollen, leaf, root system, color, and even the branching structure are copied directly from nature and are remarkably realistic. Today's botanically correct florals look, feel, and are as flexible as real flowers. You may need to touch them to prove they are not fresh.

While botanically correct flowers and many botanical-like flowers tend to be expensive, they can be the focal point of a bridal bouquet or reception arrangement that uses less expensive accent flowers. Also consider that top-quality florals are long lasting and can be kept as precious wedding mementos or reused in your home décor.

Line flowers   Mass flowers   Form flowers   Accent flowers

Flower Roles

Flowers play certain roles in a hand-held bouquet or table arrangement, based on their shapes and sizes. Once you understand the roles of flowers, you can use a design shown in this book and substitute similar flowers that suit your wedding theme and color preferences.

Line flower. Shaped like a spike or having a long stem, a line flower establishes the height and width of the arrangement. Examples are gladiolus, larkspur, snapdragon, and liatris.

Mass flower. This is a single, large, round flower that adds bulk and texture to a design. Examples are peonies, hydrangea, open garden roses, and ranunculus.

Form flower. A form flower has a distinctive shape that attracts the eye and gives interesting visual texture to the arrangement. Examples are lilies, callas, orchids, lisianthus, alstroemeria, anthuriums, and birds-of-paradise.

Accent flower. Also called "filler flowers," these flowers accent the spaces between the main flowers in a design and are usually added last. They include gypsophila, caspia, statice, and wax flower.

COLOR

The color scheme is often the first decision most couples make about their wedding, and many other plans center around that choice. You might select certain colors because they relate to the season of the year or simply because they are your favorites.

The color wheel shows the relationships between colors and can help you choose colors that work well together. The twelve basic colors are arranged by how they are created and how they relate to each other. Red, yellow, and blue are called primary colors because they are not made from other colors. Orange, green, and violet are called secondary colors. Each is made by combining equal amounts of two primary colors. For example, red plus yellow equals orange. The two-name colors (red-orange, and blue-violet) are called tertiary colors. They are made by combining one primary color and one secondary color in equal or unequal amounts. Warm colors (red, orange, yellow) tend to dominate other colors and may seem to project out from a design. Cool colors (green, blue, and violet) are calm and restful. They tend to blend into the background.

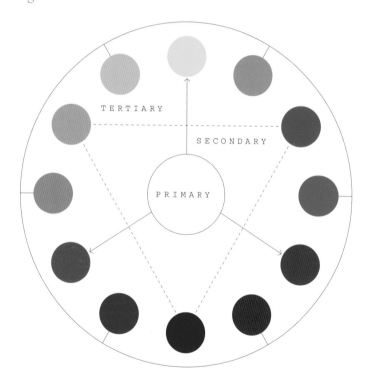

As you plan the colors for your wedding florals, use the color wheel to help you anticipate how certain combinations of colors will look. Here are some of the possible color schemes you might use.

| Monochromatic | Analogous | Complementary | Triadic |

Monochromatic. This color scheme uses various intensities of one color. In the bouquet shown here, four different kinds of flowers are combined with sparkling beads in various shades of blue. In monochromatic arrangements, textures are important.

Analogous. An analogous design uses colors that are next to each other on the color wheel. For example, this corsage in a silver holder, called a tussy mussy, uses blue, blue-violet, and violet flowers.

Complementary. This scheme uses colors located on opposite sides of the color wheel. The pink ranunculus and green hydrangea in this flower girl bouquet complement each other very nicely.

Triadic. This scheme uses three colors that are the same distance apart on the color wheel, such as the three primary colors of this ring bearer's truck arrangement.

TOOLS AND MATERIALS

Tools and materials for creating beautiful faux floral wedding designs are available in craft stores, from florists, and wherever high quality faux flowers are sold. There are also Internet sources for specialty products, such as the Smithers Oasis bouquet holders and pew clips and the Lomey Design System for constructing elegant table arrangements. These products, designed to be sturdy, practical, and easy to work with, are the same ones used by professional florists.

Knife (1). A large, sharp knife works well for cutting foam, and a smaller sharp knife is used for shaping foam. Choose a knife that feels comfortable in your hand. Sharpen knives after each use, and keep them in a toolbox or other safe place.

Scissors (2). You need these for cutting ribbon, foliage, fabrics, paper, or other items that do not contain metal. Sharpen your scissors regularly.

Shears (3). This is a very useful tool for cutting small wires and wired ribbon and does not need to be sharpened.

Utility snips (4). Snips are often needed to cut thick stems, branches, and wire.

Awl (5). This sharp, pointed metal rod is used for poking holes in firm materials.

Wire cutters (6). This tool is used to cut wires and faux floral stems and has blades shaped for cutting close to the stem.

Tape measure (7). Keep this handy for measuring foam size, stem lengths, and design proportions.

Bouquet stand. Whenever you work on a bouquet or pew clip design, mount the holder in a bouquet stand or a clamp secured to the work table. Then both hands are free to design the arrangement at the proper angle and height.

Tack 2000 (1). This multipurpose spray adhesive provides a strong, acid-free bond. An adjustable nozzle controls the spray pattern, and the spray stays sticky long enough that you don't have to rush.

Lomey adhesive (2). Used to secure the plastic pieces of the Lomey system, this adhesive dries quickly but must set for 24 hours before florals can be added. Read and follow the manufacturer's directions carefully.

Glue pan (3). This small electric skillet (not deep-fat fryer) is used to melt glue pillows.

Pan glue pillows (4). These nuggets or blocks of adhesive are melted in a glue pan. Don't mix with glue sticks; also, don't mix glues from different companies, as the chemical composition is different and the mixture may not adhere.

Paintbrush (5). A small, inexpensive natural bristle paintbrush with a wooden handle can be used to apply glue to items too large or awkward to dip in the pan.

Small clay saucer (6). When placed in the glue pan, this saucer keeps the brush from resting on the bottom of the pan where it could burn.

Glue gun (7). A hot glue gun can be used to secure items when a glue pan is too awkward. The high-temperature variety is best for faux florals.

Glue sticks (8). Sticks used for the glue gun are available with white, clear, and glittered glue. Choose the type recommended by the manufacturer of your glue gun.

Floral wire (9). This is used to bind floral materials together and to lengthen stems that are too short for the design. Wires are 18" (46 cm) long and sized in gauges from 16 to 28; the smaller the number, the thicker the wire. A 24-gauge wire is versatile for faux floral designs.

Wood picks (10). These thin pieces of wood with a point on one end and a thin wire on the other come in green, brown, and natural. They are used to secure ribbon loops, extend stems, and secure foam inside a basket. The 6" and 9" (15 and 23 cm) lengths will fill most of your needs.

Wax string (11). This is used for tying garland to a banister or to secure a floral design to a chair post without marring the wood.

Floral tape (12). Self-sealing, tape in greens, browns, white, and rainbow colors is used in floral design to wrap wires and lengthen stems.

Anchor tape (13). Used for securing foam to a base, this tape on a roll is available in green, white, or clear. The ½" (1.3 cm) width is used for large projects and the ¼" (6 mm) width for small designs.

Anchoring Materials

Styrofoam (1). This plastic foam has a hard or rough surface and is sold in white, greens, and browns. Styrofoam is available in various sizes and shapes, such as hearts, squares, orbs, cones, wreaths, and crosses. It is used for thick-stemmed florals and materials on picks.

Dried floral foam (2). Sold in blocks, sheets, wreaths, and shapes and available in greens, browns, and brights, dried floral foam is easily cut with a knife. It grips stems securely and won't melt when glue is applied.

Candle stakes (3). These small plastic holders with long spikes for inserting into foam are available in sizes to fit tapers and pillar candles.

Lomey Design System (4). This unique product line includes pedestals, columns, saucers, rim pads, universal pieces, foam cages, and special glue. Like Tinkertoys for the floral designer, the parts go together in infinite ways to create floral arrangements in many shapes and sizes.

Wedding Belle bouquet holder (5). Dried floral foam in a dome-shaped cage is attached to a round plastic handle. The holders are available in different sizes, with straight or slanted handles that can be ribbon-wrapped or tucked into a decorative sleeve.

Lomey bouquet holder (6). Dried floral foam in a flat, round cage is attached to a flat plastic handle. The holders are available in different sizes, with straight or bent handles that can be decorated.

Elegant bouquet holder (7). Dried floral foam in a dome-shaped cage is attached to a decorative handle with a silver or gold finish.

Bravo holder (8). Dried floral foam inside a plastic tube can be used upright to hold stems for a bouquet or turned sideways with flowers inserted at both ends.

Mini-Deco holder (9). Dried floral foam dome with a self-stick bottom is useful for small arrangements, such as cake toppers or flourishes on ring bearer pillows.

Pew clip with foam cage (10). Plastic clip fits over a pew end or chair back. A foam-filled cage is attached to the front.

Decorative weights (11). Marbles, sea glass, stones, and rocks, in a variety of colors, sizes, and shapes, can be used to add physical and visual weight and a decorative accent to table designs.

Crystal fiber (1). These fine, tangled, synthetic fibers have an opalescent look that adds shimmer and sparkle to floral designs. Crystal fiber is available in different colors.

Corsage leaves (2). Available in a variety of sizes, shapes, textures, and colors, these wired fabric leaves are used as bases or accents for corsages and boutonnieres.

Lace cake topper (3). This molded plastic container, usually covered with lace, is made to hold a small floral design for decorating the top of a wedding cake. Foam must be cut to fit inside the topper. Small projections around the base give it a foothold in the frosting.

Flower dye (4). Flowers can be tinted nearly any color desired using this translucent dye in an aerosol spray. The dye comes out very light for applying pastel shades and can be intensified with more layers. Read the manufacturer's directions.

Corsage and boutonniere pins (5). Corsages are held in place with two pins, which usually have a pearl or tear-shaped head and are 2" to 2½" (5 to 6.5 cm) long. Boutonnieres are secured with one pin, usually 1½" (3.8 cm) long with a black or white ball head. White pinheads can be colored with flower dye.

Wire accents (6). Silver or gold curled wire forms, often embellished with rhinestones or pearls, are used to give sparkling details to corsages, boutonnieres, favors, or cake toppers.

Bouquet handle covers (7). Plastic bouquet handles can be covered with a simple padded satin sleeve. For a more decorative look, there are handle covers in different colors and styles, some with beads, tassels, or metallic effects.

Wired beads (8). To dress up floral designs, glass and plastic beads in lots of colors and shapes can be bought as individual wired stems, multiple branches on one stem, small wreaths, or garlands with many branching stems.

Ribbons

Ribbons bring romance and beauty to a wedding. Whether tied in lavish bows, wound through garlands, or hung in breezy streamers, ribbons add lots of color and texture. They range in width from 1/16" (1.5 mm) to 4" (100 mm) and come in a wide variety of colors and styles.

Woven-edge ribbons are manufactured in a wide range of widths, with various surface textures and weave styles that add special touches to personal flowers. Styles include single-face satin, which is lustrous on one side and matte on the other; double-face satin, which is lustrous on both sides; and sheer. Any of these styles may also come with fine wires woven into the edges to help shape the bow loops and streamers.

Cut-edge ribbons are manufactured as wide synthetic fabric and then cut with special knives that heat-fuse the edges. They are generally less expensive than woven-edge ribbons, making them useful for multiple bows on pew decorations or garlands. One side is usually lustrous and the other side matte, though both sides can be exposed in a bow to offer more visual texture.

Candles

Choose high-quality candles that are dripless, long-burning, and non-smoking for your wedding designs. It is a good idea to avoid candles with fragrances, especially at the reception where their scents can compete with food aromas and flavors and may cause allergic reactions for some of the guests. Here are a few more tips on candle care and use.

- Trim wicks to ¼" (6 mm) to keep the flame low and prolong the burning time. This may also prevent some candles from smoking.

- Protect surfaces with candle holders. Always use candle stakes for inserting candles into foam. If candles are inside glass containers, make sure flames will not come in contact with glass.

- Keep the candle flame away from combustible material and out of reach of children.

- Store candles in a cool place, away from direct sunlight.

- Remove all wrapping and labels from candles before lighting, including any labels on the bottom.

- Do not burn candles for more than three or four hours at a time. Follow instructions specific for each type of candle.

- Use a candle snuffer to extinguish a candle to prevent excessive smoking and possible splattering of the wax. If you must blow out the candle, place your index finger in front of the flame and gently blow on your finger. The air will travel around your finger, meet on the other side, and extinguish the candle. It not only looks chic; it keeps wax from splattering on the tablecloth. Never extinguish a candle with water, as this could cause splattering of the wax.

- To remove wax from linens, first freeze the fabric and break away as much of the wax as you can. Then stretch the fabric over a sink, and pour boiling water from a teakettle over the stain. Wax can be removed from upholstery and carpeting by placing a paper towel or brown paper bag over the wax and running a warm iron over the paper.

TECHNIQUES

Preparing a Shopping List

Make a list of all the faux floral projects you want to make. If the floral materials used in the book don't fit your color scheme, or if the projects don't coordinate with each other, choose different flowers for the project recipes according to their roles. Take a preliminary "window shopping" trip to help you make selections.

Before buying the materials, make a chart, listing the projects down the left side with columns for each floral ingredient across the top. Enter all the ingredients for each project. In many cases you will need the same flowers for several projects. Be specific about size, style, and color. Then tally the ingredients at the bottom of the page. When you go shopping, buy all the materials at once to be sure of getting them alike. Check each stem to be sure it hasn't lost any blossoms or leaves. Planning and shopping for your floral materials in this way saves you time by eliminating multiple trips to the store. You may receive discounts for buying florals in large quantities, and you'll also have everything at hand when you start your projects.

Preparing Florals

When you buy faux florals, they may look flat and lifeless from having been packed tightly in boxes. So before you put them into a design, you need to fluff every flower and leaf. Remove the price and information tags, and bend and shape the stems. Open up the flowers and arrange the leaves in a natural way.

Many floral materials also need to be reinforced so the flower heads won't separate from the stems later. This is particularly true when the head and leaves have been made separately and slipped over the stem. Check the flower parts. If they aren't securely fastened, remove those parts. Apply hot glue to the peg on the stem and put back the leaf or flower. Allow the glue to set before you work with the material. If you take this step, you'll prevent flowers and leaves from falling off during the wedding.

Cutting Stems

Always cut a floral stem at a sharp angle using a wire cutter. The point makes it easier to insert the stem into foam and takes up less space. When the instructions say to cut a certain number of inches from the stem, that always means from the bottom of the original, main stem. Sometimes the directions say to cut the stems to a certain length, measured from the top flower to the stem end.

Often a faux floral stem has several flowers, as well as foliage. The instructions may say to cut the stem into pieces. Find a section in the main stem that has a long distance between smaller branches. Cut the main stem at an angle just above the lower branch, as shown at right. This will give the upper stem the length it needs. The flower at the end of the lower stem now tops the newly cut stem. If it is necessary to disguise the cut, touch up the area with paint to match the stem color. Often leaves can be bent or turned to hide a cut.

Wrapping Floral Wire

Floral wire is often wrapped with tape to make it easier to handle and less visible in the arrangement.

1 Hold the end of the tape at the top of the wire. Twirl the wire in one hand while you wrap it with tape in spirals, moving down the wire. Overlap the tape slightly and leave no gaps.

2 At the bottom of the wire, tear the tape. Seal the tape to the end of the wire by rolling the wire between your fingers.

Lengthening a Stem

Sometimes you need to lengthen a stem so it will work in your design. Perhaps you've cut a stem into pieces, and some of the pieces just aren't long enough. You can easily extend a stem with wire.

1 Cut a floral wire as long as the present stem plus the length you want the stem to be extended. Hold the wire alongside the faux floral stem.

2 Wrap floral tape around the calyx (base of the blossom), gently stretching the tape and pressing the tape onto itself. Floral tape is a reversible strip of crepe paper coated with wax on both sides. As the tape stretches, the wax is released to secure the floral tape to the stem. The warmth of your fingers softens the wax, causing the tape to stick to itself.

3 Twirl the floral stem with one hand while stretching and warming the tape between the thumb and index finger of the other hand. The tape spirals around and down the stem, covering the stem and wire together. The tape should overlap each wrap, with no gaps. However, too much tape gives a bulky, unnatural appearance.

4 When you run out of floral stem, continue wrapping to the bottom of the wire. Then tear the tape from the roll (it's not necessary to cut it). Seal the end of the tape to the end of the wire by rolling the stem in your fingers.

Inserting Stems

To create the projects in this book exactly the way they are shown, the instructions tell you to insert stems into the foam in certain places. Each stem insertion actually requires the following steps:

1 Cut the stem to the length described in the instructions. This measurement includes the depth to which the end will be inserted, usually 2" to 3" (5 to 7.5 cm). Or determine the length desired by holding the stem in place and adding the insertion length.

2 Trim away any foliage or flowers that are in the 2" to 3" (5 to 7.5 cm) above the stem end.

3 Insert the stem into the desired place to check it once more before gluing.

4 Dip the end of the stem into the glue pan so a generous amount of glue sticks to the stem. Or apply glue with a hot glue gun. Immediately place the stem into the hole and hold it in place for a few seconds.

Many of the designs are created by first orienting the foam or holder like the face of a clock, with the top or back at 12:00 and the front or bottom at 6:00. This refers to the way the item will be viewed. For a bouquet, the clock numbers refer to the way the flowers will be viewed by others, not by the person holding it. The stem insertion directions are given as positions on the clock, so they are easy to understand.

Working with Styrofoam and Dry Floral Foam

Before you cut the foam, sketch the desired shape. You can cut with a sharp knife. When cutting Styrofoam with a knife, run the sharp blade edge into the side of an old candle before each cut, to help the knife cut smoothly and make less noise. Make sure you cut with the sharp edge directed away from your body. To remove loose particles, rub the pieces together. A cautionary note: Do not expose foam to flames or intense heat during storage, design, or final use.

Using a Glue Pan

A glue pan works at a lower and more variable temperature than a glue gun. Place the pan on a piece of hard plastic to protect your work surface. When you turn off the glue pan, you can keep the glue in it until next time. Set the temperature so the glue is liquid but not smoking. There are two ways to apply the glue to materials.

Dipping. Floral foam and faux floral stems can be dipped into the glue pan before you secure them.

Brushing. When an object is too large or awkward to dip, you can transfer glue from the pan with a small paintbrush.

Using a Glue Gun

A glue gun is the best way to apply glue directly to a design. Heat the gun, place the tip where you want the glue, pull the trigger, and move the gun in a circular motion, ending with an upward movement to break off the glue. The glue will be hot; if you aren't careful, you can get a nasty burn. Also, when the glue is hot, it will ooze out of the gun at a touch of the trigger, so please be careful. Rest the glue gun on a nonflammable surface when not in use.

Making a Multiloop Bow

The following method keeps the lustrous side of the ribbon facing outward and the matte side hidden inside the loops.

1   Cut 9" (23 cm) of 24-gauge wire and set it aside. Unroll about a yard (meter) of ribbon, but don't cut it. Grasp the ribbon between your left thumb and index finger, with the shiny side facing up; leave a tail of the desired length below your hand.

2   Make a sharp half twist in the ribbon at the point where you are grasping it, and hold the twist between your thumb and finger; the matte side is now facing up above your hand.

3   Bring the ribbon down over your thumb in a small loop, wrapping the ribbon flat against the twist on the underside; slip it between your thumb and finger. The matte side will again be facing up above your hand.

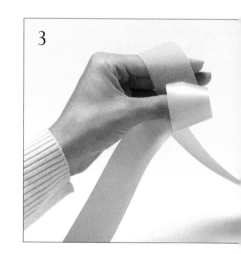

3

4   Make a sharp half twist in the ribbon again at the point where you are grasping it, and hold the twist between your thumb and finger. The shiny side will now be facing up above your hand.

5 Turn under the ribbon, forming a loop above your hand and bringing the matte side flat against the twists on the underside. Slip the ribbon between your thumb and finger. The matte side will now be facing up below your hand.

6 Make a sharp half twist in the ribbon again at the point where you are grasping it, and hold the twist between your thumb and finger. The shiny side will now be facing up below your hand.

7 Turn under the ribbon, forming a loop below your hand, bringing the matte side flat against the twists on the underside; slip it between your thumb and finger. The matte side will now be facing up above your hand.

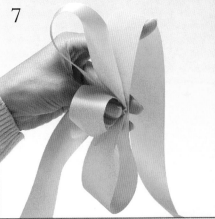

8 Repeat steps 4 to 7 at least twice or until you have made the desired number of loops. Make each pair of loops the same size or slightly larger than the pair above them.

9 Give the ribbon a final half twist and slip the twist between your finger and thumb with the other twists. Cut the ribbon at an angle, leaving a tail of the desired length.

10 Insert the wire (from step 1) through the thumb loop so the middle of the wire rests under your thumb and the end comes out between your index and middle finger.

11 Bend the wire ends down so they are parallel to each other and perpendicular to the back of the bow. Press the top of your right index finger tight against the underside of the bow between the wires. Holding the wires with the other fingers and palm of your right hand, remove your left thumb and index finger.

12 Grasp the bow loops with your left hand and turn them twice, so the wires twist tightly between your right index finger and the bow back. Release the loops and give them a fluff.

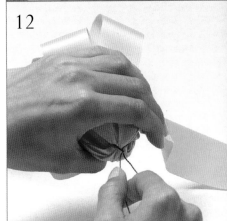

If the bow will be used in a bouquet, tie it with a length of ribbon instead of the wire. This will prevent scratching the person carrying the bouquet. For pew or chair decorations, use pipe cleaners for tying bows to protect the wood.

Making Streamers

1 Drape one, two, or several ribbons (depending on their width) over your hand, leaving streamers of the desired length.

2 Bring the ribbon up to your hand once or twice, forming deep loops. The loops can be slightly shorter than the streamers and, if more than one, slightly different from each other. Hold all the ribbons together in your hand. Cut the ribbons from the reels, leaving streamers of the desired length. Angle-cut the ends.

3 Tie the ribbons together where they cross your hand, using another length of ribbon or a floral wire.

4 If fewer loops and more streamers are desired, cut one or two of the loops.

5 Tie simple overhand knots (love knots) or tiny shoe-lace bows in some of the streamers at various heights to create texture and movement.

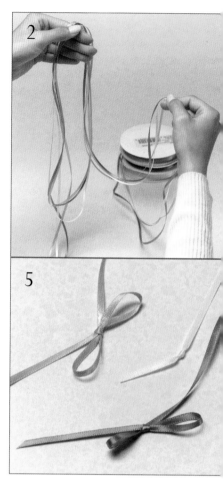

Three Flowers in a Bud Vase

This basic design concept is used in arranging florals in a bouquet or table design. The first three floral elements may be arranged in this way, establishing the shape of the arrangement. Or clusters of florals within a design may be grouped in this way. The first flower, usually a bud or the smallest flower, is cut to a length at least one and one half times the height of the container. The second flower is three-fourths the height of the first one and placed either to the right or left of the first flower. The third flower is three-fourths the height of the second and placed on the opposite side of the second flower.

Bouquet Size and Proportion

The bride's bouquet should be the right size and proportion for her and for the style and fullness of her gown. A slender sheath gown would be overpowered by a large presentation bouquet just as an extravagant bouffant ball gown would dwarf a scepter bouquet. A good guideline is to measure the bride from one inner hip bone to the other for the bouquet width and from her navel to her knees for the length. There are no hard-and-fast rules, however, and much depends on the bride's preference.

Checking and Adjusting

When you have completed your design, step back and look it over. One of the best ways to see what others see is to look at the design in a mirror. The mirror takes away a dimension and shows you what the camera sees. Here are some things to check.

• Are the flowers where you want them? Some may have been pushed out of place while you were designing. Each flower deserves its own space. Gently move the main flowers if they are touching one another.

• If you have cut stems, are the cuts concealed? Is the foam covered?

• Do you see any glue or glue strings? Set a hair dryer on hot, and run the air slowly over the design to melt away any glue strings.

• Are you happy?

Packaging and Labeling

One of the main benefits of using permanent botanicals is that you can design at your leisure, weeks or months before the wedding. Carefully packaging and labeling items as you finish them keeps them intact, clean, and organized. Choose large boxes to hold and protect several related items, such as centerpieces, favors, or boutonnieres. Cushion the bottom of the box with decorative packing material, such as crumpled tissue paper or shredded cellophane, to keep items apart and to prevent the florals and ribbons from crushing. Use smaller, decorative boxes, perhaps clear plastic or white cardboard with cellophane viewing panels, for items that will be presented individually to members of the wedding party or special guests—bouquets, mothers' corsages, ring bearer's pillow, or a flower girl's baskette. Along with the label, add a personal note, if desired, and tie the box with a ribbon. Be sure to include the person's entire name and role in the event.

Make a list of all the floral items for the wedding, from the largest altar arrangement to the smallest boutonniere. Include information on when it is to be delivered, exactly where and how it should be placed, to whom it will be presented, including the full name and role. Assume the person who reads the instructions has no idea what to do with the package. Make sure all packages have appropriate information. Make several copies of the final list: one for the bride, one for the mother of the bride, one for the person who will distribute the flowers, one for the person in charge of decorating the reception site, one for the personal attendant. This saves a lot of wedding day confusion.

Bridal Bouquets

Cascade Bouquet of White Orchids

The cascade bouquet is a formal design, often selected when the bride wears a gown with a train. Like a gentle waterfall, the flowers of a cascade bouquet drape gracefully over the left wrist and down into a flowing garland below. Large cymbidium orchids are the focus flowers, with stems of smaller dendrobium orchids creating the long trailing line of the cascade. Other white flowers and loops of satin ribbon provide a variety of textures. All the stems are inserted into foam in the top of a silver bouquet holder.

FLORALS

- Chinese evergreen leaves: one large, four medium, three small
- Two stems white dendrobium orchids with three branches each
- Six white cymbidium orchids
- Two stems white freesia with three branches and foliage on each
- One stem white lisianthus with two flowers and a bud
- Four stems stephanotis with multiple blossom clusters on each

TOOLS AND MATERIALS

- Elegant bouquet holder (page 16)
- Bouquet stand or clamp
- Dark green floral tape
- Several 18" (46 cm), 22-gauge wires
- Wire cutter
- 2½ yd. (2.3 m) white satin double-face ribbon, 1½" (39 mm) wide
- Scissors
- 6" (15 cm) wired wood pick
- Glue pan and glue pillows
- Glue gun and glue sticks

1 Place the bouquet holder upright in a stand or clamp. Visually orient the bouquet holder like a clock face. Insert the largest Chinese evergreen leaf near the base of the foam at 6:00, a medium leaf at 1:00, the others around the outside of the holder, forming a collar to hide the mechanics and foam from the back.

2 Cut the dendrobium orchids into three stems each so you have two long, two medium, and two short stems. Insert the two longest stems and one short stem into the holder at 6:00, 7:00, and 5:00, respectively, radiating from the bouquet center. Insert the two medium stems and the remaining short stem at 1:00, 1:30, and 2:00 to drape out over the left wrist. Note that both of these groupings follow the "three flowers in a bud vase" arrangement (page 26).

3 Lengthen two cymbidium stems (page 22) to 10" and 8" (25 cm and 20.5 cm). Cut the remaining four stems 4" (10 cm) long and wrap them with floral tape. Insert the orchids so they form a cascading line through the center of the bouquet from the top left (11:00) to the bottom right (4:30). The longest stems should be at the bottom. The lip (forward edge of the innermost petal) of the orchid should always point toward the center of this bouquet.

Tip *Faux floral stems are wire covered with vinyl. Some, like these cymbidium orchids, are very smooth and may spin in the holder, even when they are glued in place. Wrapping the stems with floral tape before inserting them into the foam helps keep them in place.*

4 Divide the lisianthus stem into a large flower with a 4" (10 cm) stem and a smaller flower and bud on a 6" (15 cm) stem. Insert the largest lisianthus deep into the foam at 12:30. Insert the smaller lisianthus and bud at 2:00, in from the dendrobium.

5 Cut each freesia stem into three pieces, measuring 8", 4", and 2" (20.5, 10, and 5 cm). Separate and shape the foliage. Insert a long, medium, and short stem halfway up the foam cage around 6:30, forming "three flowers in a bud vase". Repeat with the remaining stems near the base of the foam cage around 9:00. Add the freesia foliage where needed.

6 Divide the stephanotis into three stems each, varying the number of blossoms and buds in each piece. Using wire and floral tape, lengthen the stems of the stephanotis pieces that do not have a long or strong stem. Insert the stephanotis bunches throughout the bouquet, using the additional foliage from the stems to fill in, add depth, and cover the mechanics.

7 Make a streamer (page 26) with 2 yd. (1.85 m) of the ribbon; attach it to a wired wood pick, and insert it into the underside of the bouquet at 6:30. Cut the remaining ribbon into 4" (10 cm) pieces. Bend each piece into a small loop and glue the loops into the bouquet at random.

7

BLUE TEARDROP CASCADE

This smaller teardrop-shaped cascade bouquet uses deep blue irises as the focus flowers. They are accented with anemones, delphiniums, and hydrangeas. Eucalyptus stems with berries and foliage are tucked in amid the flowers. Inserted at the top back of the bouquet is a multiloop bow with long tails (page 24) that drape over the bride's wrist.

33

Crescent Bouquet of Tropical Florals

A crescent bouquet is shaped in a gentle, asymmetrical arc, with most of the flowers draping to the bride's left and outward. This design, secured in a large plastic holder, features tropical flowers in bright exotic colors. The correct way to carry a bouquet made in this holder is with the handle parallel to the floor and the cage tilted upward, not with the handle down as you might expect. This way, the bride is better able to control the weight of the bouquet and keep it from drooping forward.

As you insert each stem in this bouquet, remember the point of radiation is the center, and all flowers and greens should look as if they begin there. Use the large spaces on the top of the foam cage as well as the narrow slots on the underside for inserting stems. Because so many stems need to fit in such a small piece of foam, cut each stem at a sharp angle, allowing about 2" (5 cm) to go into the foam.

FLORALS

- *Three small birds-of-paradise*
- *Four small green anthuriums*
- *Two paphiopedilum orchids*
- *Two tropical leaves*
- *One stem oncidium orchid*
- *Two stems green hanging amaranthus*
- *One stem violet dendrobium orchid*
- *Two stems green bouvardia*
- *Two stems eucalyptus berry with foliage*

TOOLS AND MATERIALS

- *Large Lomey bent-handle bouquet holder*
- *Bouquet stand or clamp*
- *Wire cutter*
- *Glue pan and glue pillows*
- *Glue gun and glue sticks*

1 Place the bouquet holder in a stand or clamp with the handle parallel to the floor and the cage tilting upward. Visually orient the bouquet holder like a clock face.

2 Remove the leaves from the bird-of-paradise stems; set aside. Cut the bird-of-paradise stems to measure 6", 4", and 2" (15, 10, and 5 cm), respectively, from the flowers. Insert the long stem at 1:00 near the bottom of the foam and the medium stem at 2:00 near the bottom of the foam, with the points of both flowers angling toward the center of the holder. Insert the short stem deep into the top of the foam cage, matching the angle of the first two.

Tip *The eye will follow where it is directed. Angling the points of the birds back toward the center invites the viewer's eyes to revisit the bouquet. Remember this technique when designing bouquets or table arrangements with flowers that seem to point, such as anthuriums, orchids, and snapdragons.*

3

3 Cut the anthurium stems 10", 7", 6", and 3" (25.5, 18, 15, and 7.5 cm), respectively from the flower. Bend the flowers so the stigmas and petal tips direct the eye back toward the center. Insert the 10" stem at 7:00 near the bottom of the foam. Insert the 7" stem above the first at 7:30, the 6" at 6:30 in the middle of the foam cage. Insert the 3" stem deep, with the back of the flower touching the foam at 8:00. The birds-of-paradise and anthuriums are directly across from each other.

4 Cut the paphiopedilum orchid stems to 6" and 4" (15 and 10 cm). Insert the long stem at 11:00, the short stem slightly lower and to the right.

5 Cut the stems of the tropical leaves to 4" and 2" (10 and 5 cm). Insert the long stem at 10:00 near the back of the foam; insert the short stem slightly above it in the same position.

6 Cut the stems of the three bird-of-paradise leaves to 2" (5 cm). Insert them at 2:00, 3:00, and 4:00 near the back of the foam.

7 Cut shorter stems from the oncidium orchid, leaving the main stem long. Insert the long stem at 3:00, draping out and down to 4:00. Insert the short stems in a grouping closer to the center of the bouquet. Allow spaces between the flowers and foliage to create depth.

8 Cut the amaranthus into separate stems and insert them in the same area as the oncidium orchids, letting them drape to the side and down for movement and texture.

9 Cut the dendrobium orchid into three stems: long, medium, and short. Insert the long stem under the 6" (15 cm) anthurium slightly to the right, the medium stem above that one and the third coming from the bouquet center.

10 Cut the bouvardia blossoms and eucalyptus berries and foliage into clusters. Insert them into the bouquet at different angles and depths wherever you need to cover foam and mechanics.

Sphere of Roses with a Wheat Halo

Traditional bouquets, sometimes called colonial bouquets, have a strong central point of radiation and a round, domed profile. This bold, dramatic design proves that traditional can also be unique. The tightly packed cluster of white roses, symbolic of true love and purity, is surrounded by a halo of golden wheat heads, in many cultures a symbol of abundance and prosperity. To protect the long, wispy beards of the wheat heads while transporting the bouquet to the ceremony, pack the bouquet in a large box resting over a soft collar of crumpled tissue paper.

FLORALS

- Two bunches of natural bearded wheat
- Seven white open roses and three rosebuds

TOOLS AND MATERIALS

- Large, Lomey bent-handle bouquet holder
- Bouquet stand or clamp
- Shears
- Glue pan and glue pillows
- Glue gun and glue sticks
- Wire cutter
- White satin bouquet holder cover with tie

1 Place the bouquet holder in a stand or clamp with the handle parallel to the floor and the cage tilting upward.

2 Remove 12 stems of wheat from one bunch. Cut the stems 1" (2.5 cm) long. Remove the beards (the long grassy strands) from the ends of these 12 stems. Set the stems aside.

3 Divide the remaining wheat stalks into two equal bunches, with the longest, sturdiest heads in one bunch. Then divide the other bunch into two equal groups, with the medium-size heads in one group and the smallest heads in the last group. Cut the stems 1½" (3.8 cm) below the heads.

4 Dip the stems of the largest wheat heads, one at a time, into the glue pan and then insert them into the foam around the base of the cage. Push the stem in, up to the bottom of the head. Form a compact row, with each head radiating from the center of the cage. If the heads are curved, insert them so they curve toward the center of the bouquet.

5 Insert a second row of wheat heads just in front of the first row, mixing medium and small heads and staggering placement to fill gaps between heads in the first row. Repeat with a third row.

6 Add the 12 heads without beards into open spaces, as needed.

4

7

7 Using angle cuts, trim the stems of the roses and buds so they are 1½" (3.8 cm) long. Insert six roses, evenly spaced, in a circle just inside the wheat. Insert the seventh rose in the center. Insert the rosebuds in open spaces at slightly different heights to make a solid mounded center of roses inside the wheat collar.

8 Place the satin handle cover over the end of the handle. Apply a drop of glue from the glue gun to four areas on the back of the large part of the bouquet holder as close as you can to the first row of wheat. Pull the satin handle up around the back close to the wheat to cover your mechanics. Tie the attached ribbon with a double knot and small bow.

PARCHMENT ROSES SPHERE

This compact sphere of pink parchment roses is the perfect bouquet for an attendant or mother of the bride. The roses are secured in a straight-handled Wedding Belle bouquet holder, beginning with five large roses in the north, south, east, west, and center positions. About 15 large and medium roses and several rosebuds fill in the spaces. A touch of glue secures the handle in an elegant velvet cover called a Posy Pocket.

Hand-Tied Bouquet

The hand-tied bouquet is one of the most popular styles today, especially for those brides who prefer a less formal, garden-style approach. This bouquet is very easy to make. Stems are held in one hand and added to the bouquet one at a time. Because the flowers are not glued in place and the stems are trimmed last, there is plenty of opportunity to make changes and perfect the bouquet arrangement.

Beaded wire loops add sparkle to this hand-tied bouquet, and the flower stems are wrapped with satin ribbon. For a personal touch, a charm that has special meaning for the bride is caught in the ribbon wrap where only she can see it.

FLORALS

- *Three stems light blue peony, each with two large leaves and a small leaf*
- *Two stems blue cosmos, each cut into four parts*
- *Two stems blue California currant, each cut into two parts*
- *Two stems blue wheat spray, each cut into two parts*

TOOLS AND MATERIALS

- *Wire cutters*
- *24" (61 cm) beaded wire with five branching stems*
- *Two 24-gauge wires cut in half*
- *Green floral tape*
- *Green anchor tape, ½" (1.3 cm) wide*
- *Charm*
- *Glue pan and glue pillows or glue gun and glue sticks*
- *½ yd. (0.5 m) white satin ribbon, 1/16" (1.5 mm) wide*
- *3 yd. (2.75 m) blue wire-edged ribbon, 1½" (39 mm) wide*
- *Scissors*

1 Remove the foliage, nodes, and branches from the cut flower parts; set aside. Arrange the florals in separate groups.

2 Bend the end of each branch of the beaded wire back to the point where it emerges from the main stem. Wrap a piece of wire tightly around the gathered ends, securing them onto the main stem. Wrap the wired area with green floral tape. Shape and arrange the five loops. This will be the center stem of the bouquet.

3 Hold the beaded stem straight up in your left hand, with your thumb on top. Place a peony across the front at an angle, with the head left and tail right. Close your thumb over the stem.

4 With your right hand above the left, grasp the stems with your right hand, then release the left. Now with the flowers in your right hand, make a one-quarter turn toward your body. Put the flowers back in your left hand.

5 Repeat steps 3 and 4 with the other two peonies. Then repeat with the cosmos stems, placing them at varied heights. Then add the currant stems and the wheat stems. Turn the bouquet each time you add a flower, foliage, or accent flower.

6 Look at the bouquet and decide if the flowers are placed where you like; pull some stems out slightly to make them more visible. Bend and shape the flower stems for a realistic garden feel. If some stems are not long enough, set them aside for now.

7 Add the six large peony leaves to the back of the bouquet under the flowers. Bend them out at a slight right angle to the bouquet handle.

8 Tightly wrap the stems with anchor tape above the hand holding the bouquet.

9 Add any shorter stems to the bouquet with glue from the glue pan. Glue the three smaller peony leaves into the center of the bouquet.

10 Hold the bouquet with one hand at the top just under the foliage; place the second hand directly below the first on the stem. Mark the spot below the lower hand and cut the stems at the mark.

11 Lace the white satin ribbon through the metal loop of the charm. Tie a knot to hold the charm in place. Place the ribbon tails alongside the flower stems at the back of the bouquet (closest to the bride), with the charm 2" (5 cm) above the point where the stems are wrapped. Tuck the charm behind a large peony leaf to hold it in place while you ribbon-wrap the stem.

12 Touch one end of the blue ribbon into the hot glue and secure it about 1" (2.5 cm) from the bottom of the stems. Wrap the ribbon over the stem ends; then turn the ribbon and begin wrapping it around the stems.

13 Continue wrapping the ribbon tightly up the stems, overlapping to cover the stems and the charm ribbons completely. Cover the floral tape at the top. Cut the ribbon and glue the end to the bouquet.

14 Cut a 12" (30.5 cm) length of blue ribbon and set aside. Make a multiloop bow (page 24) with the remaining ribbon. Instead of wiring, tie it with the 12" (30.5 cm) length of ribbon and use the tails to tie the bow around the handle, just under the leaves at the front of the bouquet. Pull the charm from the peony leaves and let it hang down onto the handle in an obvious place for the bride to see.

FLORAL WRAP VARIATION

Instead of a ribbon wrapping, cover the stems and create a billowy collar for the bouquet with 1½ yd. (1.4 m) of 20" (51 cm) white mesh floral wrap. Make the bouquet, following steps 1 to 11. Round the corners of the mesh and fold them to the center. Place the stem bottoms in the center of the mesh and gently twist the mesh around the stems. The mesh will curve itself into a collar around the base of the bouquet. Secure the mesh high under the bouquet with clear anchor tape. Tie a 24" (61 cm) length of ribbon over the tape; knot it, and tie a small shoe bow. Pull the charm into view.

Garden-style Presentation Bouquet

This lovely "fresh from the garden" gathering of flowers is carried with the stems in the left hand and the flowers resting over the left forearm and bent elbow. In this French carriage style, the flower heads are supported by the left hand, with the right hand resting over the stems. Bare stems are part of the design in a presentation bouquet, so look for flowers that have natural-looking stems, or you can wrap less attractive stems with green floral tape or ribbon. For wedding photos, the flowers, never the stems, should be turned toward the camera to ensure that pictures capture the full beauty of a presentation bouquet.

FLORALS

- Eight stems leatherleaf fern, each with seven branches of foliage
- Five stems snapdragons
- Four stems lilies with one flower and two buds each
- Two stems stock
- Three stems parchment hydrangea
- One stem lady's mantle with three branches
- Six stems statice

TOOLS AND MATERIALS

- 3 yd. (2.75 m) wire-edged sheer peach ribbon, 1½" (39 mm) wide
- Green anchor tape
- Scissors
- Wire cutter
- Glue gun and glue sticks

1 Cut 1 yd. (0.92 m) ribbon for a tie. Make a multiloop bow (page 24) from the remaining ribbon; tie the bow with the ribbon tie. Set aside.

2 Place one full leatherleaf stem on the work surface. Place a second full stem to the right, crossing the first stem just below the leaves (point of radiation). Place the third full stem to the lower left, crossing the first two stems at the point of radiation. The ferns will form a triangle.

3 Place a snapdragon over the center fern, so the flower stalk tip is about 4" (10 cm) beyond the fern tip. Place a second snapdragon over the second fern and a third snapdragon over the third fern, each extending like the first.

4 Place one lily stem to the right of the first snapdragon, one to the lower left, and the third lower than the second lily to the right, like "three flowers in a bud vase" (page 26). Place the fourth lily on the lower left. Bend and shape the stems of the flowers to add depth, but maintain the established shape.

5 Add the last two snapdragons to the lower right and left, each at a 45° angle. Remember all of the flower stems must meet at the point of radiation.

6 Add the stock stems to the bouquet wherever more texture and depth are needed.

7 Insert one hydrangea into the right side of the bouquet, between the top lily and the lower snapdragon. Insert the other two hydrangeas close in at the base, just above the point of radiation.

8 Cut the remaining leatherleaf stems just above the lowest two leaf branches, making five five-branch stems and five two branch stems. Holding the bouquet gently in one hand, add the divided leatherleaf foliage to any open places. Use glue if necessary.

9 Cut the lady's mantle stem into three parts, leaving one long stem and two shorter stems. Insert the stems into the bouquet where you want more texture.

10 Insert the statice stems throughout the bouquet for added texture.

11 Look over the bouquet and make any necessary adjustments. Check the overall shape and depth. When you are satisfied, secure the stems at the point of radiation with the green anchor tape.

12 Cut the stems at various lengths, from 12" to 6" (30.5 to 15 cm). Tie the bow over the floral tape, under the hydrangeas.

PRESENTATION BOUQUET OF BRILLIANT CALLAS

Create a striking presentation bouquet with nine callas, adding stems of spiral eucalyptus for color contrast and texture. Bend and shape each calla stem into a gentle crescent, the stem to your left, flower to the right, opening upward. Secure the stems with a ballet ribbon wrap. Begin at the bottom with ribbon tails of equal length. Bring the tails around to the front, and crisscross them tightly twice. Wrap the tails to the back and crisscross them tightly twice. Continue this way to the top of the stems, and knot the ends. Finish the bouquet by adding a multiloop bow.

Duchess Rose Scepter

A traditional bouquet might not appeal to the bride who likes to think outside the box. This contemporary scepter bouquet features a queen-size composite rose atop a curvy, wire-wrapped stem. A composite flower is made by separating the petals of two or more blossoms and reassembling them into one extravagant fantasy flower. Crisscrossed wires orbiting above the flower add to the excitement. Though simple to craft, the Duchess Rose makes a dramatic statement.

FLORALS

- *Three open standard red roses on long stems with leaves*

TOOLS AND MATERIALS

- *Newspaper*
- *Cardboard disc, 3" (7.5 cm) in diameter with 1" (2.5 cm) center hole*
- *Moss green flower dye*
- *Tack 2000 spray adhesive*
- *Glue pan and glue pillows*
- *Glue gun and glue sticks*
- *Green floral tape*
- *4 yd. (3.7 m) golden cream wire-edge ribbon, 1½" (39 mm) wide*
- *Shears*
- *Wire cutter*
- *8 yd. (3.7 m) red decorative 24-gauge wire*

1   Cover the work surface with newspaper. Color both sides of the cardboard disc with moss green flower dye (page 18). Allow it to dry completely.

2   Cut the stems from the rose leaves and remove the plastic veins on the back. Spread the rose leaves facedown on the newspaper. Apply Tack 2000 spray glue to the leaf backs.

3   Arrange the leaves on the disc, beginning on the outside edge and working toward the center in a spiral. Cover the entire side, leaving the center hole open. Repeat on the other side. Allow the glue to dry completely. Choose the prettier side for the bottom, as the rose will cover the top.

4   Remove the flower from one stem. Remove the calyx (the green part). Touch the stem end in hot glue, and replace the flower on the stem. Remove the leaves from the stem. Set the stem aside.

5   Remove the flowers from other stems and set the stems aside. Remove the calyxes (the green parts at the base of the flower) from the blossoms. Cut each petal from the rose at the base. Cut any white or light parts from the base of the petals.

6   Dip the cut end of one petal in the hot glue and secure it to the top of the leaf-covered disc near the outer edge. Repeat with a second petal, overlapping the first one slightly. Continue attaching petals, working in a spiral pattern until the disc is covered. Leave the center hole open.

7   Gently insert the stem of the whole rose through the center hole until the head of the flower nestles into the petals. Adjust the position as necessary. Raise the center rose, apply hot glue to the bottom, and lower it back in place. Hold it for a moment to allow the glue to set.

8   Place the two reserved stems alongside the primary stem. Wrap them tightly together with floral tape, forming one main stem.

9 Cut the ribbon in half. Cut a 6" (15 cm) piece from one length, and set it aside. From the rest of that ribbon length, make a multiloop bow (page 24) with 10" (25.5 cm) tails. Use the short length to tie the bow. Set aside.

10 Touch one end of the remaining ribbon in the hot glue, and fold the end over the bottom of the rose stem. Wrap the ribbon tightly up the stem, stopping under the leafed disc; glue in place with hot glue gun.

11 Cut several pieces of decorative wire 9" (23 cm) long; curve them into arcs. Dip the ends in glue, and secure them in the Duchess Rose in various positions, creating depth and making a canopy over the flower.

11

12 Wrap the stem with the remaining wire, up and down the stem over and over until you run out of wire. Glue the end where it stops.

13 Tie the bow under the disc. Secure in place with a touch of hot glue.

LILY SCEPTER

Other composite flowers, such as this large lily, can also become scepter bouquets. Choose any flat leaves to cover the disc base. Here slender pointed leaves give the design a starburst effect. White lilies were tinted with Just for Flowers translucent spray color (page 18). A ballet ribbon wrap (page 49) punctuated with white pearl corsage pins accents the scepter handle.

Bridal Party Accessories

Half a Dozen Boutonnieres

Boutonniere, a French word meaning button-hole, is the name of the flower worn by the men in the wedding party and other significant males; such as the fathers and grandfathers of the bride and groom. A boutonniere is worn on the left lapel, where suit jackets once had buttonholes, and it is attached with a single bead-headed pin or a magnet. The boutonniere is a single medium-sized flower or a cluster of up to three small flowers. The groom's boutonniere usually echoes the flowers in the bride's bouquet, in keeping with a legend that tells of the bride clipping a flower from her bouquet to give her groom on their wedding day. The flowers worn by the groomsmen coordinate with the bridesmaids' bouquets, and those worn by fathers and grandfathers use flowers similar to those in their partners' corsages.

The red rose boutonniere with a natural stem is a classic choice that works well for many wedding floral themes. Each flower and leaf is wired and taped, similar to the way fresh floral boutonnieres are made. This makes them more pliant and natural than a plain faux stem. These basic steps can be followed with a different flower that coordinates with the bride's bouquet.

FLORALS

- *One red rose*
- *One rosebud*
- *Rose leaves cut from stems*

TOOLS AND MATERIALS

- *Wire cutter*
- *Glue pan and glue pillows*
- *Glue gun and glue sticks*
- *Candle and match*
- *Five 22-gauge wires, 9" (23 cm) long*
- *Dark green floral tape*
- *Two pieces of wired rhinestone trim*
- *1½" (3.8 cm) boutonniere pin*

Classic Red Rose

1 Cut the rose and bud stems to 2" (5 cm) long. Remove the rose blossom from the stem. Dip the attaching point into glue, and reattach the blossom. Repeat for the rosebud.

2 Light the candle. Hold the end of a wire in the flame. When the wire is hot, push it through the calyx (the green part at the base of the blossom) of the rose. Pull the wire halfway through and bend the ends down alongside the stem. Repeat with a second wire, pushing it through perpendicular to and slightly below or above the first wire.

3 Wrap the stem and wires together with floral tape, beginning just below the calyx, moving upward to cover the calyx, and then down to the end of the wires. Set aside.

4 Repeat steps 2 and 3 for the rosebud.

5 Form the last wire into a hairpin shape. Slip the wire around the stem junction of the rose leaves where the two lower leaves are attached to the main stem. Pull the wire ends down alongside the stem until the bend in the wire hugs the stem junction. Wrap the stem and wires together with floral tape, beginning at the junction and covering all of the wire.

6 Place the taped rose leaves to the back of the bud. Secure them together with a couple wraps of floral tape.

7 Place the larger rose below and to the right of the bud. Secure them together with a couple wraps of floral tape.

8 Place the wired rhinestone trims behind the leaves on the upper right and lower left. Wrap all the stems together the full length of the wires.

9 Cut the stem 1½" (3.8 cm) below the calyx of the large rose. Cover the cut end with floral tape.

Tip *Choose floral tape to match the flower stems or blend with the tuxedos. Tape comes in dark green, light green, brown, black, and white. Boutonniere pins have a bead end available in black, white, and a rainbow of colors. Black, the most popular, is very formal and best used with black tuxedos. White-headed pins can be used universally. Colored pins can be chosen to match the flowers.*

Tiny but powerful magnets, available where wedding craft supplies are sold, are a great way to hold boutonnieres in place. One magnet is hidden inside the ribbon-wrapped stem of this single calla. The opposite magnet side goes under the lapel. No need for pins! The ribbon-wrap technique is also perfect for tulips.

FLORALS

- *Calla*

TOOLS AND MATERIALS

- *Wire cutter*
- *Candle and match*
- *One 26-gauge wire, cut in half*
- *Floral tape*
- *Magnets*
- *Glue gun and glue sticks*
- *5" (12.7 cm) satin double-face ribbon, 1½" (39 mm) wide*
- *Scissors*

Wrapped Calla

1 Cut the calla blossom, leaving the stem ½" (1.3 cm) long. Light the candle. Hold the end of a wire in the flame until the wire is hot, and then push the wire through the base of the calla. Pull the wire halfway through and bend the ends down alongside the stem. Repeat with a second wire, pushing it through perpendicular to and slightly below or above the first wire.

2 Wrap the stem and wires together with floral tape, beginning at the base of the blossom, moving upward to cover the wires, and then down to the end of the wires. Cut the taped stem 1½" (3.8 cm) long.

3 Separate the magnet parts; set the silver part aside. Bend the wires of the gold part into U shapes, so the ends rest alongside each other on the back of the magnet in a figure eight. Glue the magnet to the back of the boutonniere, with the wires at the top and bottom.

4 Secure one end of the ribbon over the stem end, using hot glue. Then wrap the stem tightly from bottom to top with the ribbon, covering the taped wires and magnet. When you reach the flower, wrap up around the flower base. Cut the ribbon at an angle and leave a tab of ribbon extending on the back of the flower. The ribbon end will be behind the flower.

5 Secure the silver magnet part to the back of the boutonniere.

Tip *If the calla is larger than you want, cut off the flower base at the desired height. Remove the stigma and shorten it to the desired length. Trim the petal, if necessary. Then roll the petal back around the stigma into its natural shape but smaller.*

Look for white gerberas that have a natural-looking fuzzy wired stem. Tint them with floral spray.

FLORALS

- *Miniature white gerbera*

TOOLS AND MATERIALS

- *Wire cutter*
- *One pearl head corsage pin*
- *Glue gun and glue sticks*
- *Flower dye*
- *Pencil*
- *Boutonniere pin*

Wreath boutonnieres, suitable any time of year, are easy to make with faux pine needles and small floral pieces.

FLORALS

- *10 to 12 long pine needles*
- *Small pieces of plumosa fern*
- *Small pieces of eucalyptus berries*
- *Small pieces of Queen Anne's lace*

TOOLS AND MATERIALS

- *30-gauge decorative silver wire*
- *Wire cutter*
- *Glue pan and glue pillows*
- *Decorative wired bead accent stem, 3" (7.5 cm) long*
- *Two decorative pearl beads*
- *Boutonniere pin*

Single Gerbera

1 Cut the pearl head corsage pin to ¼" (6 mm). Glue the pearl head into the center of the flower.

2 Tint the gerbera to the desired color and intensity, using flower dye, if necessary.

3 Cut the stem of the gerbera to 4" (10 cm), using a wire cutter. Twist the stem around a pencil to curl it. Turn the cut end toward the back and bend the flower head forward slightly.

Miniature Wreath

1 Remove the long pine needles from the base stem. Lay them side by side, in different directions, staggering the ends to make a bundle about 9" (23 cm) long. Taper the thickness in the last 2" (5 cm) of each end.

2 Wrap the needles tightly together with silver wire, moving up and down the bundle four times. More and tighter wraps make the bundle more pliable and colorful. Stop wrapping near one end, but do not cut the wire.

3 Form the bundle into a small wreath, overlapping the ends 2" (5 cm). Wrap the overlapping ends together and continue to wrap the entire wreath twice around the circle. Add a touch of hot glue, if necessary.

4 Pierce the wreath from top to bottom with the decorative wire accent stem. Add two beads to the end, and secure with glue.

5 Cut small pieces of the eucalyptus berries, Queen Anne's lace, and plumosa fern. Glue them here and there around the wreath.

Simple, tasteful boutonnieres are easy to make using metal pin-on cones.

FLORALS

- *Hydrangea*

TOOLS AND MATERIALS

- *Dark green floral tape*
- *Scissors*
- *Glue gun and glue sticks*
- *Metal cone with pin back*

Ribbon-wrapped scepter stems add a bit of panache. The same ribbon and flowers used in the wedding party bouquets can be used in tailored, masculine boutonnieres.

FLORALS

- *Three sweet pea flowers with leaves*

TOOLS AND MATERIALS

- *Wire cutter*
- *Candle and match*
- *Six 26-gauge wires, 6" (15 cm) long*
- *Dark green floral tape*
- *6" (15 cm) ribbon, ½" (12 mm) wide*
- *Scissors*
- *Glue gun and glue sticks*
- *Two boutonniere pins*
- *One bead*

Silver Cone with Hydrangea

1 Remove two blossoms and a small leaf from a hydrangea. Place the leaf behind the blossoms, and wrap all the stems together with floral tape.

2 Remove two or three petal layers from another blossom. Glue the petals over the taped stems.

3 Apply a small amount of hot glue to the inside surface of the cone. Insert the wrapped stems, with the leaf toward the back (pin side) and the blossoms resting on the cone rim.

Sweet Pea Scepter

1 Cut a bud, two medium-sized flowers, and four leaves from the sweet pea stem, leaving the stems 1½" (3.8 cm) long.

2 Light the candle. Hold the end of a wire in the flame. Push the hot wire through the bud calyx. Pull the wire halfway through and bend the ends down alongside the stem. Wrap the bud stem and wires together with floral tape, from the calyx to the end of the wires.

3 Repeat step 2 for the flowers, catching a leaf stem into the wrap, just under each flower.

4 Arrange the stems like "three flowers in a bud vase" (page 26). Tape all together with floral tape. Cut the stem 2" (5 cm) long.

5 Glue one end of the ribbon over the cut end. Then wrap the stem tightly from bottom to top with the ribbon. Glue the ribbon end behind a leaf at the back.

6 Run a boutonniere pin through a bead and up into the stem, making sure the tip stays inside the ribbon wrapper. Secure with a touch of glue.

Carry Corsage of Gerberas

A modern way to honor a mother or grandmother of the bride or groom is with a small bouquet called a carry corsage. The design shown is made with white gerberas that have been tinted a cheerful sunshine yellow. Though it looks as if the flowers are merely held in a tight bouquet, the blossoms are actually cut from the stems and inserted into floral foam in the top of a bouquet holder. The bare stems of the gerberas surround the plastic handle and are wrapped with dainty Dior bows. A similar effect could be achieved with other large blossoms on straight stems, such as mums, open roses, peonies, or dahlias.

FLORALS

- Nine white gerberas
- Ten medium leaves

TOOLS AND MATERIALS

- Flower dye
- Safety glasses
- Nine pearl head corsage pins
- Wire cutter
- Newspaper
- Tack 2000 spray adhesive

- Wedding Belle bouquet holder
- Glue pan and glue pillows
- Glue gun and glue sticks
- Two rubber bands
- Shears
- 1 yd. (0.92 m) wired ribbon, 1½" (39 mm) wide

1 Cut the stems of the gerberas 2" (5 cm) long; reserve the long stems.

2 Tint the gerberas a soft yellow with the flower dye. Intensify the color to your taste. Allow to dry for 30 seconds. The fragrance will dissipate in a short time.

3 Put on the safety glasses. Angle-cut the corsage pins ½" (1.3 cm) below the pearl, using a heavy-duty wire cutter. Touch the sharp end of each pin into the glue and place it in the center of a gerbera.

4 Cut the stems from the ten leaves. Remove the plastic veins from the backs of the leaves. Place the leaves facedown on newspaper. Spray with adhesive. Adhere the leaves to the underside of the bouquet holder.

5 Dip the short gerbera stems into the glue pan; then insert them into the foam of the holder, using the north, south, east, and west insertion pattern. Push the stems in until the backs of the flowers touch the foam. Add the remaining flowers in the open places.

6 Cut the reserved gerbera stems into 6" (15 cm) pieces, using a wire cutter. Gather them together and wrap tightly with one rubber band 2" (5 cm) from the top and the other rubber band 2" (5 cm) from the bottom.

4

5

7 Cut the ribbon into two 9" (23 cm) lengths, two 6" (15 cm) lengths, and two 3" (7.5 cm) lengths. Touch one end of a 6" ribbon in the glue; wrap it around the stem covering the top rubber band; secure the other end with glue. Repeat with the other 6" length around the lower rubber band, gluing the ribbon ends directly below the top ones.

8 To make a Dior bow, place a 9" ribbon on the work surface and fold in the ends so they overlap slightly in the center; secure with glue. Wrap the 3" piece around the center, keeping the bow flat, not gathered; glue the ends in place. Repeat for the second bow.

9 Glue the bows onto the handle, covering the lapped ribbons.

8

10 Touch the bouquet handle in the hot glue, and insert the handle gently and quickly into the center of the clustered stems.

VIOLET TUSSY MUSSY

This sweet little corsage is carried in a purchased silver tussy mussy holder that later can be propped into its own special stand at the reception. The flowers are arranged following the general directions for a hand-tied bouquet (page 42) and then all the stems are wrapped together with floral tape. The flowers include sweet peas, lisianthus, anemone, African violets, and wax flowers.

Corsage of Garden Stems

The bride and groom honor their mothers, grandmothers, and other special female relatives or friends with a corsage to wear throughout the ceremony and reception. Customarily the corsage is worn on the left shoulder, attached with corsage pins or magnets to the outer clothing. To be comfortable, a corsage must be as lightweight as possible, so care is taken to use light florals, ribbons, and other materials. Flowers must be medium or small, never large.

This garden stem corsage features individually wrapped, natural-looking stems. It has a mass flower (rose), two form flowers (morning glories), and accent flowers (wax flowers). This formula can also be used with different flowers.

FLORALS

- One stem wax flowers
- Two small morning glories with buds
- One small rose with a bud
- One large ivy leaf

TOOLS AND MATERIALS

- 24" (61 cm) ribbon, 1½" (39 mm) wide
- Several 26-gauge wires cut into 9" (23 cm) pieces
- Green floral tape
- Candle and match
- Wire cutter
- Scissors

1 Make a five-loop bow (page 24), about 4" (10 cm) wide, with 4" (10 cm) tails. Secure the center with wire. Wrap the wire ends together with floral tape from the base of the bow to the ends. Set aside.

2 Divide the wax flower into one stem with three blossoms and one stem with one blossom and leaves. Separate the individual morning glory blossoms and bud and the rose blossom and bud. Cut all the flower stems 2" (5 cm) long.

3 Light the candle. Hold the end of a wire in the flame until it is hot, and then push the wire through the calyx (the green part at the base of the blossom) of a morning glory. Pull the wire halfway through and bend the ends down alongside the stem. Wrap the stem and wires together with floral tape, beginning at the calyx. Repeat for the other morning glory, the rose, and the rosebud. Set aside.

4 Form a wire into a hairpin shape. Slip the wire over the bottom wax flower branch and pull the wire ends down alongside the stem until the bend in the wire hugs the connecting point. Don't twist the wires. Wrap the stem and wires together with floral tape, beginning at the bend in the wire. Repeat for the remaining stems. For single, non-branching stems, place a wire alongside the stem and wrap the stem and wire together with floral tape.

3

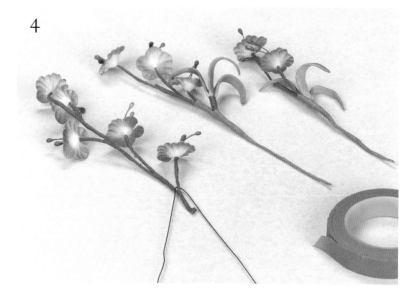

4

5 Form a wire into a hairpin shape. Heat both ends of the wire in the candle flame. Push both ends through the front of the ivy leaf, straddling the center vein ½" (1.3 cm) above the leaf base (a). Pull the wire ends down alongside the leaf stem until the bend in the wire hugs the leaf (b). Wrap the stem and wires together with floral tape, beginning at the leaf base (c).

6 Hold the ivy leaf in one hand. Place the morning glory bud on top of it with tips even. Add the rose bud slightly lower and to the right. Add a wax flower stem slightly lower and to the left, resembling "three flowers in a bud vase" (page 26).

7 Place one morning glory over the stems to the right. Place the other morning glory slightly lower and to the left. Place the rose between and slightly below the morning glories. Add a three-blossom wax flower stem into the center and arrange the blossoms so they drape out and down.

8 Place the bow over the stems and just below the lowest flower. Wrap floral tape five times around all the stems and ribbon wires, just under the bow. Keep the stems separate and natural.

9 Cut the stems at various lengths; twist the floral tape at the cut end of each stem to hide the wire. Spread the stems out to resemble a natural bouquet. Bend the flowers slightly away from the leaf and turn their faces forward.

Katarina's Bouquet

This unique bouquet can be carried by the rounded top handle or the small scepter stem. It is for a flower girl or a junior bridesmaid. I have named the design after my dear friend and

talented floral designer Katarina Lusvigsson from Sweden, who taught me how to make it. This is also a wonderful chair back decoration and can be made in a smaller version for a wedding favor.

FLORALS

- *One stem ranunculus with three flowers, two buds, and eight leaves*
- *One large parchment hydrangea*
- *One stem wax flower, cut into eight parts*
- *Five large hydrangea leaves*

TOOLS AND MATERIALS

- *4 yd. (3.7 m) pink- and green-striped ribbon, 1½" (39 mm) wide*
- *Ribbon scissors*
- *Two 21-gauge wires*
- *Glue gun and glue sticks or glue pan and glue pillows*
- *Floral tape*
- *Four 24-gauge wires*
- *Wire cutter*
- *Candle and match*

1 Cut a 6" (15 cm) piece of ribbon for a bow tie; set aside. Cut another piece of ribbon 3 yd. (2.75 m) long and make a ten-loop bow with a center loop and 6" (15 cm) tails (page 24). Tie the center with the reserved 6" ribbon.

2 Wrap the two 21-gauge wires together with floral tape. Cut a 12" (30.5 cm) length of ribbon. Apply a drop of glue to one end of the joined wires. Fold one end of the ribbon over the glued end. Then turn the ribbon and wrap it in a tight spiral around the wires, completely covering them. Secure with glue at the other end.

3 Bend the ribbon-wrapped wires into an oval so the ends cross. Wrap the ends together tightly with an 18" (46 cm) 24-gauge wire, leaving two wire tails of equal length. Cover the intersection with floral tape and continue wrapping the wires together to the end. This forms the rounded handle.

4 Cut the stem of the hydrangea to measure 5" (12.7 cm). Place the handle in the center of the hydrangea. Wrap the handle and hydrangea stem together with floral tape.

5 Cut three 24-gauge wires in half. Bend each of the wires into a tight U shape. Cut the stems from the hydrangea leaves, but keep the veins on the leaf backs. Light the candle. Heat both ends of a bent wire in the candle flame. Push the hot ends through the front of the leaf, straddling the center vein ½" (1.3 cm) above the leaf base. Pull the wire ends down alongside the leaf stem until the bend in the wire hugs the leaf. Wrap the stem and wires together with floral tape, beginning at the leaf base. Repeat with the other four leaves.

3

5

6 Bend back each hydrangea leaf to a right angle. Tuck the leaves under the hydrangea, forming a collar around the blossoms. Wrap the leaf stems together with the main stem, using floral tape.

7 Cut the main stem 6" (15 cm) long; wrap floral tape over the end. Wrap the stem with ribbon, as in step 2, securing the end with glue to the underside of a leaf.

8 Orient the top of the bouquet like a clock face, with the handle horizontal in the center. Glue the first large ranunculus at 11:00, the second at 1:00, close to the foliage collar, and the third at 7:00 facing up. Glue one bud in the center and the other halfway between the collar and handle at 5:00.

9 Glue the wax flower blossoms and ranunculus foliage here and there into the bouquet for added color and texture.

10 Glue the bow high under the foliage collar. Glue the two back loops together on the side opposite the center loop, so the bow wraps completely around the main stem.

HANDLE CHOICES

A young flower girl may find it easier to carry Katarina's bouquet by the ribbon-covered handle at the top, similar to the way she would carry a small basket. For older girls who would have no trouble holding the bouquet upright by the scepter handle, the top handle can be shaped into a heart.

Ribbon-Wrapped Baskette

The ingenious design of the Bravo floral foam holder makes it easy to create unique wedding accents of all kinds. In this design, the tube is turned sideways, wrapped with ribbon, and accented with small floral bundles in each end. With the addition of a ribbon handle, it can be carried down the aisle by a flower girl or bridesmaid or hung as a chair back or pew decoration. Select ribbon and flowers to match the wedding theme. The little nosegays of paper roses are especially convenient to use, and they come in many colors.

FLORALS

- Two nosegays of miniature paper roses with leaves, 12 flowers each
- One stem blue larkspur with 13 flowers, three buds, and foliage

TOOLS AND MATERIALS

- Scissors
- 1¾ yd. (6 m) yellow- and blue-striped brocade ribbon, 1½" (39 mm) wide
- Small Bravo floral foam holder (page 17)
- Plastic drinking straw
- One pipe cleaner
- Pencil
- Glue pan and glue pillows
- Glue gun and glue sticks
- Wire cutter

1 Cut 16" (40.5 cm) of ribbon for the handle. Cut three 7" (18 cm) pieces to wrap around the foam holder. Cut 9" for the Dior bow, 3" (7.5 cm) for the bow center, 5" (12.7 cm) for the long streamer, and 3" (7.5 cm) for the short streamer. Set the pieces aside.

2 Push the drinking straw through the foam close to one inside edge of the holder. Cut both ends of the straw ½" (1.3 cm) beyond the ends of the foam holder. Fold the pipe cleaner in half, catching one end of the ribbon handle in the fold. Insert the pipe cleaner ends into the straw, and gently pull the ribbon through the straw.

3 Tie the ribbon handle ends together; cut the ends close to the knot and touch the knot with glue. Pull the handle until the knot hugs one end of the straw. The straw will be at the top of the holder. Mark a pencil line on the center front of the holder.

4 Wrap one 7" (18 cm) ribbon around the holder, aligning one edge to the end of the holder and overlapping the ends at the pencil line. Secure the overlapping ends of ribbon to the holder and each other with a touch of glue. Wrap a second piece at the opposite end and the third piece in the middle, overlapping all the ribbon ends at the pencil line.

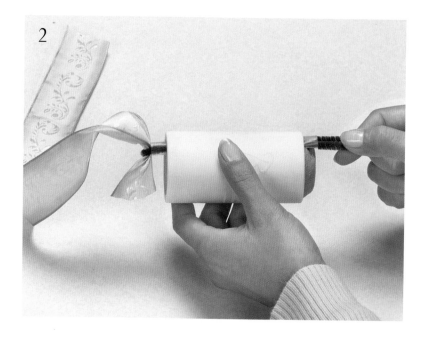

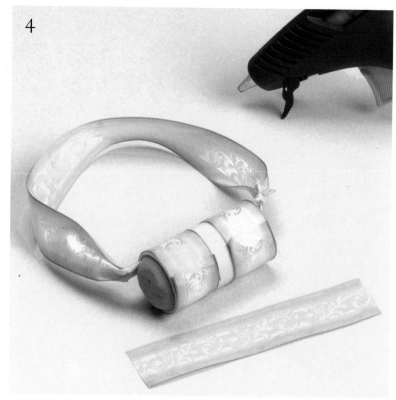

5 Cut an inverted V into one end of each ribbon streamer. Glue the straight end of the long streamer to the front center of the holder. Glue the short streamer over the long one. Make a Dior bow (page 65, step 8). Glue the bow to the holder center over the streamers.

6 Cut the stems of the larkspur blossoms and buds to 1½" (3.8 cm). Insert six blossoms around the outer edge at each end of the holder. Insert the buds here and there.

7 Cut the stems of each nosegay at an angle just below the point where they are wrapped together. Insert a nosegay of paper roses into the center of each end. Add larkspur leaves here and there for texture. Glue a larkspur blossom in the center of the bow; glue a rose, cut from one nosegay, into the center of the larkspur.

Tip *For a quick and easy way to coordinate your flower girl's shoes to her baskette, hot-glue tiny parchment roses around the openings of the shoes.*

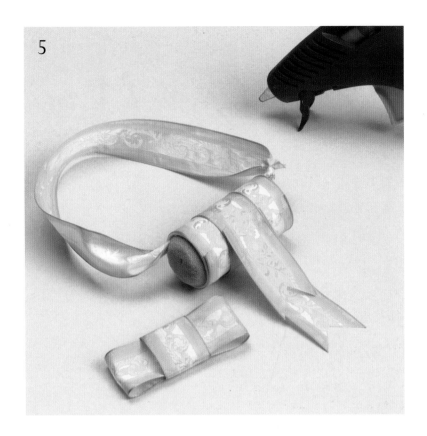

5

Flower Girl Wand

Tinkling bells announce the entrance of your flower girl as she begins her promenade. The bells are attached to ribbon streamers that dangle from her magic wand. At the tip of the ribbon-wrapped wand, a single rose rests in a puff of tulle. You could use any flower that the bride has in her bouquet. Your flower girl will treasure this charming wand as a keepsake of your wedding and the day she felt like a princess.

FLORALS

- *One large open rose with a long stem*
- *One rosebud*
- *Leaves reserved from the rose stem*

- *Two hyacinth stakes, 12" (30.5 cm) long*
- *Three white satin leaves, 2½" (6.5 cm) long*

TOOLS AND MATERIALS

- *Wire cutter*
- *Floral tape*
- *4 yd. (3.7 m) double-face satin ribbon in desired color, 1½" (39 mm) wide*
- *Scissors*
- *26-gauge wire, 6" (15 cm) long*

- *Glue gun and glue sticks*
- *3½ yd. (3.2 m) tulle, 6" (15 cm) wide*
- *6 yd. (5.5 m) sheer white ribbon with satin edges, ⅜" (9 mm) wide*
- *Two bells, 1½" (3.8 cm) wide and tall*

1 Cut the rosebud, leaving a 1½" (3.8 cm) stem; set aside. Cut the thorns, bumps, and foliage from the rose stem. Place a medium-sized three-leaf stem just below the flower, and wrap the rose and leaf stems together from the calyx to the bottom of the leaf stem with floral tape.

2 Make a three-loop bow (page 24), using 2 yd. (1.85 m) of the wide satin ribbon; leave long tails. Secure the bow with the wire.

3 Hold the bow ½" (1.3 cm) under the rose calyx, and hold the wire ends down alongside the rose stem. Wrap the entire stem and wires together with floral tape.

4 Place the two hyacinth stakes alongside the rose stem, and secure with a few wraps of floral tape. Then wrap the stem and stakes together with floral tape from the base of the flower head to the bottom of the stakes, forming the scepter.

5 Apply a small amount of glue to the end of the scepter. Fold one end of the remaining satin ribbon over the scepter end. Then fold the ribbon sideways and wrap it diagonally up the scepter. Secure it with a touch of glue at the top.

6 Glue the two large satin ribbon loops together on the side opposite the center loop, so the bow wraps completely around the top.

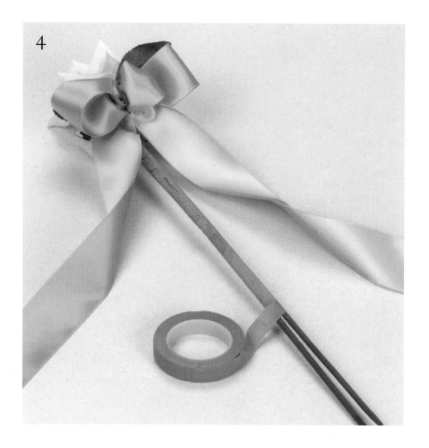

7 Make a multiloop bow with the tulle, about 8" (20.5 cm) in diameter. (It is not necessary to twist the tulle with each loop.) Fold 4 yd. (3.7 m) of narrow sheer ribbon in half, and tie the center of the tulle bow tightly with the doubled ribbon, leaving two long streamers and a long loop. Using the streamers, tie the tulle bow between the satin bow and the rose.

8 Tie the remaining sheer ribbon to the scepter, high under the satin bow, leaving tails of equal lengths. Ballet-wrap (page 49) the ribbon around the scepter to the bottom. Tie the tails in a shoe bow at the bottom. Touch with glue to secure.

9 Glue in the rosebud between the large rose and the tulle bow. Remove the wire stems from the white leaves, and glue them in close around the rose at 12:00, 4:00, and 8:00. Tie bells to the ends of the sheer streamers.

7

Sweet Wreath Headpiece

Ivy vines are easily shaped into circles and are perfect bases for headpiece wreaths for flower girls, bridesmaids, or the bride herself. Floral wreaths made the same way can also be placed on pews, chairs, or doors at the ceremony or reception or used as candle rings on reception tables. As a headpiece, the wreath can be worn across the forehead hairline and about an inch above the ear or it can be made smaller to fit around an upswept hairdo. Measure the head of the person who will wear the wreath and add ½" (1.3 cm) to accommodate the fullness of the flowers. Ribbon streamers can be added at the back of the wreath for color and movement.

FLORALS

- One or two ivy vines
- One larkspur stem
- One sweet pea stem
- Gypsophila (dry or faux)
- One or two stems wax flowers
- 24 small foam roses

TOOLS AND MATERIALS

- Two 26-gauge wires
- Floral tape
- Wire cutter
- Glue gun and glue sticks
- 3 yd. (2.75 m) each of three or four narrow ribbons in colors to match wreath flowers
- Scissors

1 Wrap the wires with floral tape and cut them in half. Measure the ivy vine to the desired length. If it is necessary to join vine pieces, overlap the ends, twist the stems together, and secure them with wire in several places. Join the vine into a wreath in the same way.

2 Cut six larkspur florets from the stem. Glue them, evenly spaced, into the wreath, placing them at various depths and angles.

3 Cut the stem of sweet peas into six parts, each with a blossom and foliage. Glue them, evenly spaced, into the wreath.

4 Cut the stem of gypsophila into small parts; glue them into the wreath on the top and sides to fill in the open places. If you want the wreath full, add more gypsophila; if you choose to have it more airy, use less.

5 Cut six small bunches of wax flowers from a stem. Glue them, evenly spaced, into the wreath. Add more bunches if you want more color.

6 Divide the 24 small foam roses into seven or eight irregular bunches. Twist the wire stems together at the base of the flowers; then bend the stems in half. Glue them, evenly spaced, into the wreath.

7 Make streamers that will fall to about elbow length, using three or four narrow ribbons (page 26). Tie them to the back of the wreath. Tie "love knots" and tiny bows at various heights in the streamers to add texture and interest.

6

7

Flourishes for Ring Pillows

Satin and lace ring bearer pillows can be purchased at craft stores and wedding departments of fabric stores. They come in several shapes, including round, square, and heart with a ribbon strap across the back for carrying the pillow and ribbon ties on the front for securing token rings. Satin pillows are easily dressed up with colorful ribbons and flowers to coordinate with the rest of the wedding florals.

Help your ring bearer learn how to carry the pillow. Have him hold his right hand palm up. Slip the pillow onto his fingers with the strap across the palm back and his thumb outside the strap. Place his left hand, palm up, under the right hand, covering the strap. If the center of the strap is secured to the pillow, have him slip one hand into each side, both palms up, with thumbs outside the strap.

For this design, blossoms are secured directly to a multiloop bow, which is then tied onto the pillow front. Select ribbon and flowers in colors to coordinate with other floral accessories.

FLORALS

- *Four oncidium orchids*
- *Three dendrobium orchids*
- *Three satin leaves, 2½" (6.5 cm) long*
- *Five small berry stems cut ½" (1.3 cm) long*

TOOLS AND MATERIALS

- *Square satin ring bearer pillow, 11" (28 cm) in diameter*
- *1½ yd. (1.4 m) wire-edge ribbon, 1½" (39 mm) wide*
- *Shears*
- *Glue gun and glue sticks*
- *Token rings*

Square Pillow

1 Cut an 18" (46 cm) length of ribbon and tie it to the point where the ribbon streamers are attached on the pillow front, leaving equal tails.

2 Make a six-loop bow with 24" (61 cm) of ribbon (page 24); tie the center with a 6" (15 cm) length of ribbon.

3 Glue the three leaves together in a triangle, satin side up, at the bases. Place a dab of hot glue in the center of the leaves, and secure them to the underside of the bow knot.

4 Cut the oncidium and dendrobium orchids, leaving 1½" to 2" (3.8 to 5 cm) stems. Touch each stem end with glue and secure it into the bow near the knot, so that flowers are positioned at various locations and angles throughout the bow. Repeat with the berry stems.

5 Tie the design onto the pillow with the 9" (23 cm) ribbon tails. Tie wedding rings to the narrow streamers, if desired.

1

4

The florals for this heart-shaped ring bearer pillow are arranged in a special Mini-Deco foam holder. Ribbon is threaded through slots on the base of the holder for tying the design to the pillow.

FLORALS

- *One stem ranunculus with one large, one medium, and one small flower*
- *24 mini foam roses*
- *10 foam trumpet lilies*
- *12 mixed-size rose leaves*

TOOLS AND MATERIALS

- *3 yd. wired sheer ribbon, 1½" (39 mm) wide*
- *Shears*
- *Mini-Deco foam holder*
- *Floral tape*
- *Glue gun and glue sticks*
- *Heart-shaped satin pillow, 11" (28 cm) wide*
- *Token rings*

Heart Pillow

1 Cut an 18" (46 cm) length of ribbon; set aside. Cut a 10" (25.5 cm) length of ribbon to use for a tie. Make an eight-loop bow, about 7" (18 cm) wide, from the remaining ribbon; tie it with the short piece.

2 Cut the stems of the ranunculus flowers to 2" (5 cm). Orienting the foam holder like the face of a clock, insert the large flower into the top right of the center, the medium one into the bottom right at 4:30, and the bud into the bottom left at 8:00.

3 Make a small nosegay of 12 of the foam roses. Wrap the stems together with floral tape, and cut them to 2" (5 cm). Insert the nosegay into the foam to the left of the large ranunculus. Insert the remaining roses into the foam one at a time in a meandering line from 1:00 to 6:00, between the ranunculuses.

4 Cut the lilies so they have 2" (5 cm) stems. Insert three lilies into the foam at 3:00, three at 6:00, and three at 11:00.

5 Thread the 18" (46 cm) ribbon through the side slots and underneath the holder. Tie the floral arrangement into the center of the bow.

6 Glue rose leaves around the base of the holder, forming a collar. Glue ranunculus leaves here and there throughout the arrangement.

7 Tie the arrangement into the center of the heart pillow, using the ring streamers. Tie rings to the ends of the streamers, if desired.

Flower-Filled Truck for the Ring Bearer

heme-oriented floral accents, like this ring bearer's truck, help small children feel comfortable in their wedding party roles. The flowers are arranged in a holder with an adhesive back and temporarily secured into the truck bed.

Token rings tied to ribbon streamers remind the young boy of the precious cargo he is carrying down the aisle. After the wedding, the floral design can be easily removed as a keepsake, and the boy can play with his new truck.

FLORALS

- Three mini gerberas
- One stem rose with a bud
- One stem wax flower with six flowers
- One stem lady's mantle with five flower clusters

TOOLS AND MATERIALS

- Mini-Deco foam holder (page 17)
- Small toy truck
- Wire cutter
- 1½ yd. (1.4 m) sheer ribbon, ⅝" (15 mm) wide
- Scissors
- ½ yd. (0.5 m) double-face satin ribbon, ¼" (6 mm) wide
- Glue pan and glue pillows or glue gun and glue sticks
- Token rings

1 Remove the paper backing from the Mini-Deco foam holder. Secure the holder in the truck bed.

2 Cut one gerbera stem 6" (15 cm) long. With the front of the truck facing you, insert the stem into the back of the foam and bend it to curve gently out of the back left of the truck, facing up. Cut the second gerbera stem 4" (10 cm) long; insert it in front of the first, bending at the same angle. Cut the third gerbera stem 4" (10 cm) long; insert it next to the first two in the back right of the truck bed.

3 Cut the rosebud stem 9" (23 cm) long; insert it between the gerberas. Bend the stem and head up. Insert the larger rose at the front center of the truck bed.

4 Make a multiloop bow (page 24) with the sheer ribbon; tie it with the double-face satin. Glue the bow to the right edge of the truck bed with the streamers hanging down. (Token wedding rings can be tied to the satin streamers just before the ceremony.)

5 Cut the wax flowers into six pieces. Cut the lady's mantle into five pieces. Glue them into the design for color and texture.

2

4

RING BEAR

Many boys think they've been asked to be the ring bear! I recall one little guy who wanted to know when he would be getting his costume. While a furry suit probably wouldn't complement the wedding theme, a young boy might feel a bit more secure walking down the aisle carrying this special bear. Make a floral sash by gluing rose leaves and small flowers to a wide ribbon. Tie the sash around the bear and knot decorative rings to the streamers.

Ceremony Flowers

Pew Cascade

Plastic pew clips with dry floral foam cages are designed to fit over the arm or back of a pew without harming the wood. Always check the ceremony site regulations to be sure clips are allowed. Before designing the cascades, take a pew clip to the ceremony site and check the fit. With the clip in place, measure how long and wide the arrangement should be so the flowers will not be in the way as guests enter and exit the rows. Pew cascades can be placed on every row, every other row, or every third row, depending on the desired look and budget. Other mass flowers, such as ranunculus or hydrangea, or form flowers, such as lilies, lisianthus, or iris, can be used instead of roses to form the cascading line through the design. Line flowers, such as tuberose or snapdragon, can be substituted for the wisteria and freesia. Following the ceremony, the cascades can be hung on chair backs at the head table.

FLORALS

- *Five parchment roses with wired stems*
- *Two branches camellia leaves, each with three stems*
- *Two stems deep violet wisteria, each with two branches and foliage*
- *Two stems freesia, each with three flowers and foliage*
- *One stem beaded berries with three branches*
- *Several stems of rose leaves*

TOOLS AND MATERIALS

- *Small Lomey pew clip with foam holder attached*
- *Bouquet stand or clamp*
- *Wire cutter*
- *Two wired wood picks, 3" (7.5 cm) long*
- *Floral tape*
- *Glue pan and glue pillows*
- *Glue gun and glue sticks*

1 Mount the pew clip in a bouquet stand or clamp, with foam holder slightly below eye level, so you will be working on it from the angle it will be seen. Orient the foam holder like a clock face.

2 Cut three rose stems 7", 6", and 4" (18, 15, and 10 cm) long; cut two stems 5" (12.7 cm) long. Insert the roses on a diagonal line from the top right to the bottom left with the longest stems at the bottom. Turn the flower heads to look up.

3 Cut one branch of the camellia foliage into one long stem and two shorter stems. Insert the longest stem in the foam at 6:00; insert the smaller ones on each side of the long stem, close to the base of the foam holder. Cut the stems from the second camellia foliage short, and insert them in and around the holder.

4 Cut three wisteria stems 18", 16", and 12" (46, 40.5, and 30.5 cm) long. From the remaining stems, cut three 8" (20.5 cm) pieces. Insert one long stem close to the back at 6:00. Insert the second stem above and to the left at 7:00. Insert the third stem to the right of the center at 5:00. Insert the short stems at 1:30, 4:00, and 7:00.

5 Cut the freesia stems into several pieces, keeping the stems as long as possible. Insert the longer stems on the sides of the arrangement, draping them down with some close to the center. Insert one or two shorter stems close to the center.

6 Remove one strand from the three-part beaded berry stem and cut it in half. Form the halves into loops and fasten the ends together with the wire of a wood pick. Insert the wood pick into the top of the cascade, forming a bow shape.

7 Loop the long remaining berry strands around and wire them to the stem base; wrap the connection with floral tape. Insert the looped stem into the lower back left.

8 Cut the rose leaf stems into small pieces. Insert throughout the design as needed.

Fan Accent with Ferns and Roses

Crisp white ribbons, open white roses, and a white lace fan are a striking contrast against dark green ferns. This design is easy to make and can be hung at the ends of pews, on chair backs, or on entrance doors. They can also be transported to the reception and used as table decorations or as accents on garlands. Smaller versions can be made as wedding favors. There are several ways to hang the fan accents. You could remove the foam cage from a pew clip and attach the fan to the clip with pipe cleaners. Fine ribbon can be threaded through the back of the fan and tied to a chair back. Or hang the fan using crossed corsage pins and a drapery hook, as for the garland on page 124, step 5.

FLORALS

- Five roses with 6" (15 cm) stems
- Two stems leatherleaf fern
- 12 lilies of the valley with 3" (7.5 cm) stems

TOOLS AND MATERIALS

- Wire cutter
- Two green pipe cleaners
- Floral tape
- 5 yd. (4.6 m) white satin ribbon, 1½" (39 mm) wide
- Scissors
- Decorative fan, 6" (15 cm) long
- Glue pan and glue pillows or glue gun and glue sticks

1 Cut each fern into two parts just
   above the bottom two branches.
Lay the two fern stems face up on the
work surface with the cut ends
overlapping 2" (5 cm). Place the center
of a pipe cleaner over the center of the
overlapped stems. Wrap twice to the left
and twice to the right, leaving the pipe
cleaner ends extending to the front.
Set aside.

2 Hold one rose in your hand; place
   another rose 1" (2.5 cm) lower.
Wrap the stems together with floral
tape. Repeat with a second set. Add a
third rose to the second set of two,
1" (2.5 cm) below the second rose.

3 Lay the taped rose stems faceup on
   the work surface, with the three-
rose stem facing left and the two-rose
stem facing right. Overlap the stems so
the roses are evenly spaced. Wrap the
stems together with floral tape.

4 Center the taped roses over the
   joined ferns. Use the pipe cleaner
ends to attach the roses to the ferns.

5 Make a six-loop bow (page 24),
   about 8" (20.5 cm) wide, with long
tails. Before tying, make two more loops
about 20" and 27" (51 and 68.5 cm)
long. Tie the bow with a pipe cleaner.

1

3

6 Attach the bow to the right of the center rose, bringing the pipe cleaner through the leatherleaf and twisting it around all of the stems.

7 Secure the open fan behind the ferns, using the pipe cleaner ends. Leave the pipe cleaner ends long for attaching to a pew, chair back, garland, or hook.

8 Glue in the lily of the valley stems and any foliage reserved from the ferns and roses.

ACCENT WITH RIBBON, IVY, AND TULLE

Sometimes gorgeous ribbon needs just a little greenery and a splash of netting to make a fabulous statement. Make a multiloop bow with extra-wide fancy ribbon, and tie it with a pipe cleaner or long twist tie, catching a couple of ivy vines on the back. Bring the ends of a 1-yd. (1 m) length of tulle together about 8" (20.5 cm) from the upper fold, and gather the layers together side to side along the overlap. Secure it to the back of the ribbon bow. Then simply attach it to a pew clip or hook and fan out the tulle above and below the bow.

Glorious Altar Display

This arrangement can be displayed on or at the foot of the altar. If your wedding is held at a park, garden, or hotel, these flowers can create a focal point behind the spot where the vows are spoken. Afterward, the design can be displayed at the reception.

The base is made of foam blocks secured to a felt-covered board, which gives the design stability and protects the surface on which it will be placed.

Though large and full of floral materials, this display is really quite easy to create by following a list and numbered diagram. Tall tapers can be added if it will be used indoors. Be sure that none of the florals will be near the flames as the candles burn down.

FLORALS

- *Five stems gladiolus*
- *Two hanging bushes, such as privit mountain bush, ivy, pathos, or a combination*
- *Five magnolia branches, each with a flower and a bud*
- *Three snowball hydrangea, each with three blossoms*

- *12 long-stem roses*
- *Five stems peony*
- *Two small ivy bushes*
- *Two grape ivy vines with grapes, each with one long and one short stem*
- *One small kalanchoe plant*

TOOLS AND MATERIALS

- *One 1 × 6 wood piece, 28" (71 cm) long*
- *Olive green felt, enough to cover the wood*
- *Staple gun and staples, optional*
- *Three blocks floral foam*
- *Green anchor tape, 1" (2.5 cm) wide*
- *Glue pan and glue pillows*
- *Glue gun and glue sticks*

- *3 yd. (2.75 m) ribbon, 1½" (39 mm) wide*
- *Scissors*
- *Six 9" (23 cm) wired wood picks*
- *Wire cutter*
- *Three 1" (2.5 cm) candle stakes*
- *Three white taper candles, 24" (61 cm) tall*
- *Green floral tape, ½" (1.3 cm) wide*

1 Cover the wood tightly with the felt, as if wrapping a gift, overlapping edges on one wide side. Secure with hot glue or staples. Glue the foam blocks, end to end, onto the side with overlapped edges. Wrap anchor tape around the foam and base at the center of each block and once lengthwise down the center. This will hold the foam in place and divide it into 12 equal sections.

1

2 Insert the following materials into the top or side of each section as numbered in the diagram above.

1 Candle stakes (three)
2 Gladiolus stem, 36" (91.5 cm) long
3 Gladiolus stem, 30" (76 cm) long
4 Gladiolus stem, 26" (66 cm) long
5 Gladiolus stem, 22" (56 cm) long
6 Gladiolus stem, 18" (46 cm) long
7 Hanging bushes (two)

8 Magnolia stems, 19" (48.5 cm) long (three)
9 Magnolia stems, 16" (40.5 cm) long (two)
10 Snowball hydrangea stems, 19" (48.5 cm) long (three)
11 Rose stems, 20" (51 cm) long (three)
12 Rose stems, 16" (40.5 cm) long (three)
13 Rose stems 12" (30.5 cm) long (three)
14 Rose stems 9" (23 cm) long (three)
15 Peony stem, 18" (46 cm) long
16 Peony stems, 16" (40.5 cm) long (two)
17 Peony stem, 14" (35.5 cm) long
18 Peony stem, 2" (5 cm) long

3 Insert the two small ivy bushes where needed to fill open spaces and cover the foam. Work the stems into the design.

4 Cut apart the kalanchoe plant. Insert the stems where color and texture is needed.

5 Cut each grape ivy vine into two stems. Insert the two short stems into the design to add texture and depth. Bend and twist the long stems with the grapes for added shape and depth, hiding the base and foam.

6 Cut the ribbon into three 1-yd. (0.92 m) lengths. Secure a wired wood pick to each length, dividing the ribbons into halves or unequal sections. Finish the ribbon ends with angled cuts or small knots, as desired. Drape and weave the ribbons into the design, inserting the picks into the foam to keep the ribbon in place.

7 Insert the candles into the candle stakes when you take the design to the ceremony site. Make sure there are no florals close to the candles.

Tip *If you will be using these flowers outdoors, it is a good idea to clamp the board to the surface under it, to prevent tipping in the breeze.*

Garden Basket for the Altar

Creamy white flowers in a blond wicker basket help lighten the usually dark area around an altar. In this easily transported design, lilies, glads, roses, and gardenias are arranged in a dramatic triangle shape that is punctuated with reedy, beaded ting ting. The tiny glass beads scattered on the ting ting catch and reflect light like rain droplets and give this casual garden basket arrangement a feeling of joyous celebration.

FLORALS

- Three stems gladiolus with foliage
- Three stems lilies with one flower and two buds each
- 10 stems calla with foliage
- 12 stems roses with foliage
- Two stems open gardenias, each with four buds and foliage
- One bunch ting ting with light green beads

TOOLS AND MATERIALS

- Basket with a handle, about 12" × 16" (30.5 × 40.5 cm)
- Enough foam to fit the basket tightly
- Four wood picks, 6" or 9" (15 or 23 cm) long
- Wire cutter
- Sheet moss
- Glue pan and glue pillows or glue gun and glue sticks

1 Place a block of foam in the center of the basket. Fill the spaces between the block and basket sides with smaller pieces of foam. Remove the wires from the wood picks. On each side of the basket, insert a wood pick through an opening in the basket into the foam. Push the picks in so the ends are flush with the outside of the basket. Place the basket on the work surface so the handle is in the center facing you.

2 Cut 2" (5 cm) from the end of one gladiolus stem, 4" (10 cm) from the second, and 6" (15 cm) from the third. Insert the longest stem in the center back of the foam. Insert the second stem 1" (2.5 cm) in front and slightly to the right. Insert the third slightly to the left in front of the second.

3 Cut 2", 4", and 6" (5, 10, and 15 cm) from the ends of the lily stems. Shape the longest stem in a slight arch and insert it into the lower left side of the foam with the flower head hanging over the edge of the basket a bit. Insert the middle stem 1" (2.5 cm) above the first, angling it to the back of the basket. Insert the shortest lily stem into the center of the foam, showing its face to the front left.

4 Cut 2" (5 cm) from the ends of three calla stems, 4" (10 cm) from the ends of four stems, and 6" (15 cm) from the ends of three stems. Shape the stems in a slight arch with the blossoms opening upward. Insert the longest stems into the lower right, draping over the basket rim. Insert the medium stems at various angles above the long ones, closer to the handle. Insert the shortest stems near the center, to the right of the handle.

5 Cut two roses 14" (35.5 cm) long, four roses 12" (30.5 cm) long, four roses 10" (25.5 cm) long, and two roses 8" (20.5 cm) long. Insert the longest roses straight up in the center, just to the right and left of the handle. Insert the shortest roses into the front of the basket, with their faces to the front, one on each side of the handle at different angles. Insert the other roses at different angles and positions on each side of the handle, filling in the triangular shape of the arrangement and giving each flower its own separate space.

6 Cut the stems of the two open gardenia flowers to 3" (7.5 cm). Insert them in the lower front on each side of the handle. Cut the stems of the gardenia buds to 6" (15 cm). Insert them at different angles around the two open gardenias.

7 Insert the ting ting stems, separately, throughout the arrangement, all angling from the central point of radiation. Keep the stems in the back as long as possible; shorten the stems at the front and sides to keep the triangle shape. Hold the stems close to the bottom and insert them gently to prevent breaking.

8 Cover any visible foam with pieces of sheet moss.

Portable Design for an Urn

Large urns that can be filled with plants or flowers are often provided at ceremony sites. This design creates a large arrangement that fits on top of an urn without harming it and is easily transported to and from the site. The flowers are arranged in groupings around a ring to achieve the look of bounty. Select a foam ring that will rest on top of the urn, with the edges overhanging the outside and inside of the lip. The urn ring can be designed at home and placed on top of the urn at the site. For added security, place double-faced clear tape around the urn lip to help hold the ring in place. Following the ceremony, the ring of florals can be removed from the urn and taken to the reception site where it can be used to decorate the buffet table.

FLORALS

- *Two stems larkspur*
- *Three stems liatris*
- *Two stems lisianthus, each with two flowers and one bud*
- *One rhododendron bush with 12 branches*
- *Two stems dahlia, each with two blooms and one bud*
- *Two heather berry stems*
- *Moss*

TOOLS AND MATERIALS

- *Styrofoam ring, 10" (25.5 cm) diameter, 2" (5 cm) thick*
- *3 yd. (2.75 m) green satin ribbon, 3" (77 mm) wide*
- *Scissors*
- *Straight pins*
- *Wire cutter*
- *Two candle stakes, 1" (2.5 cm) wide*
- *Two taper candles, 18" (46 cm) tall*
- *Glue pan and glue pillows*

1 Wrap the inner and outer edges of the Styrofoam wreath with ribbon, aligning the ribbon edge to the upper rim and allowing it to extend below the wreath. Secure with pins in several places. Place the wreath on the urn to help you keep the design in proportion.

2 Orient the wreath like a clock face. Leave one stem of the larkspur as long as possible, and insert it into the top back at 11:00. Cut 2" (5 cm) from the stem of the second larkspur, and insert it 1" (2.5 cm) in front of the first, parallel to the first.

3 Cut 2", 4", and 6" (5, 10, and 15 cm) from the liatris stems. Insert the longest stem into the top of the foam at 1:00, the medium stem to the left of the long stem, and the shortest stem to the right. Keep them vertical and parallel to each other.

4 Cut the lisianthus stems apart, leaving the bud stems 10" and 14" (25.5 and 35.5 cm) long, one flower stem 8" (20.5 cm) long, and three flower stems 6" (15 cm) long. Gently curve the bud stems, and insert them parallel to the larkspur at 11:00. Insert the longer flower stem between the bud stems, leaning the longer stem toward the front. Insert the shorter flower stems outside the buds, curving out and back.

5 Cut the candle stake legs to 2" (5 cm) and glue them into the foam at 6:00.

3

5

6 Cut six long hanging branches from the rhododendron bush. Insert the first branch into the wreath at the base of the larkspur, and trail it clockwise on top of the ring and secure with pins in several places. Insert the second branch where the first one ends, and continue covering the top of the ring. Repeat on the outside of the ring with two more long branches. Hang the fifth branch from the front at 6:00; the sixth trailing down the side from under the lisianthus at 11:00.

7 Cut the rest of the rhododendron bush into separate stems, each long enough to go firmly into the foam. Insert them wherever needed to cover the foam.

8 Cut each dahlia stem into a single flower stem and a stem with a flower and bud. Insert all the stems, one on top of the other, at 5:30. Bend and shape them to cascade out over the edge.

9 Cut the heather berry stems to 4" (10 cm); fluff and separate them. Drape one at 9:00 spilling out over the lip in front of the rhododendron. Insert the second one on top of the first.

10 Cover any visible foam and stem insertion points with moss. Insert the candles at the site.

Garden Roses Unity Candle

Many couples light a unity candle during their wedding ceremony. The arrangement includes two tapers and a pillar candle. The tapers, which represent the bride and groom, are lit early in the ceremony, often by the couple's parents. Together the bride and groom lift their tapers to light the pillar candle, symbolizing the union of their lives. The garden roses unity candle is designed on a Styrofoam heart base, so it can be made ahead of time and easily moved to the ceremony without disturbing the placement of the candles.

FLORALS

- *Seven open garden roses*
- *Four standard carnations*

- *Five small foam roses*
- *One ivy branch with two long, two medium, and two short stems*

TOOLS AND MATERIALS

- *13 yd. (12 m) white satin ribbon, 1½" (39 mm) wide*
- *Scissors*
- *Two 1" (2.5 cm) candle stakes*
- *One 3" (7.5 cm) candle stake*
- *Open Styrofoam heart, 16" (40.5 cm) diameter*
- *Seven white-tipped boutonniere pins*

- *Glue pan and glue pillows or glue gun and glue sticks*
- *One 26-gauge wire, cut in half*
- *Wire cutter*
- *Two 18" (46 cm) taper candles*
- *One pillar candle, 12" (30.5 cm) tall, 3" (7.5 cm) diameter*

1 Wrap the tops of the candle stakes with ribbon pieces, securing them with glue. Cut the points of the stakes slightly shorter than the thickness of the heart. Insert one small candle stake halfway down the left side; insert the other small stake slightly lower on the right side. Insert the large stake in the center of the top point.

2 Cover the inner edge of the top point with a 6" (15 cm) piece of ribbon; pin in place with a boutonniere pin at each end.

3 Wrap the heart tightly with ribbon, beginning at the back of the lower point and continuing all the way around. Secure with occasional touches of glue on the back of the heart. Wrap as close as possible to the candle stakes.

4 Make a multiloop bow (page 24), about 6" (15 cm) wide, with 2 yd. (1.85 m) of white satin ribbon; secure it in the center with wire. Glue the bow to the heart point at the base of the large candle stake.

5 Cut each of the flower stems to 2" (5 cm). Cut the medium and short ivy stems into smaller pieces. Glue a garden rose in the center of the bow. Working from behind the bow around the candle stake counterclockwise, glue flowers and foliage facing out and up in this order: carnation, garden rose, foam rose, garden rose, foam rose, carnation, ivy leaves, and foam rose.

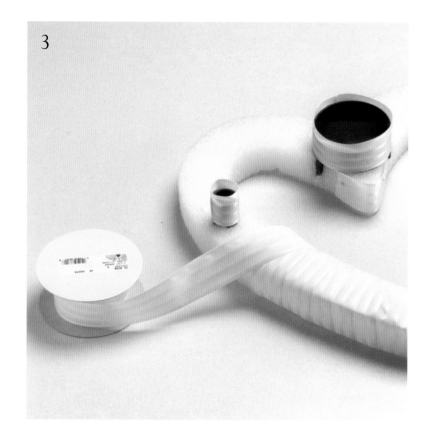

3

7

6 Glue a garden rose to the base of the right taper holder at 4:00. Moving clockwise, glue flowers in this order: foam rose, garden rose, carnation, and ivy leaves.

7 Glue a carnation to the base of the left taper holder at 4:00. Working clockwise, glue flowers in this order: garden rose, foam rose, garden rose, and ivy leaves.

8 Insert a long ivy stem beneath each of the taper holders and extend the ivy to the bottom point of the heart. Touch the ivy with glue to keep it in place. Insert the rest of the ivy in and round the three candle stakes.

9 Insert the candles into the holders at the ceremony.

Mrs. Ernest Olson

Reception Flowers

Magnolia and Rose Garland

Garlands are festive and dramatic. They add color and texture around the altar, above doorways, and over table skirting. Several garlands joined end to end can dress up an arbor. Two flower girls can walk down the aisle side by side carrying a garland between them. When you use faux florals, garlands are surprisingly easy to make. Faux floral garlands come in 6-ft. (1.85 m) lengths and are available in many styles, from simple ivy garlands to combinations with several different leaves and florals. Two or three simple garlands can be twisted together for a fuller, more interesting look. Small wreaths, nosegays, or single flowers can be added to plain garlands. Sheer or satin ribbons and bows provide a joyful finishing touch.

For ease in transporting and hanging the garlands, make garlands in 6-ft. (1.85 m) sections; then join them together as you hang them.

FLORALS

- One 6-ft. (1.85 m) rose garland with 16 roses and foliage
- One 6-ft. (1.85 m) magnolia garland

TOOLS AND MATERIALS

- Brown floral tape
- Wire cutter
- Three 26-gauge wires
- Two 24-gauge wires
- Bright-colored ribbon for marking bow placement

- 1½ yd. (1.4 m) wired sheer ribbon, 3" (77 mm) wide or 1 yd. (0.92 m) satin ribbon, 1½" (39 mm) wide, for each bow
- Corsage pins, four for each point of attachment
- Small drapery hooks, one for each point of attachment

1 Wrap all the wires with floral tape (page 22). Cut the 26-gauge wires into four pieces each; cut the 24-gauge wires into three pieces each.

2 Place the garlands side by side on the work surface and twist them together. Join them in 12 places with the 26-gauge wires, beginning in the center and moving out to the ends.

3 Make multiloop bows (page 24) from the ribbon of your choice, allowing the tails to pool on the floor. Tie them with the 24-gauge wires, leaving the wire tails long. Arrange the bows as desired along the garland. Tie a piece of the bright-colored ribbon to mark the position of each bow. Package and label the bows and garlands separately.

4 At the ceremony or reception site, attach the bows to the garland as marked, securing them with the wire tails. Mix the garland into the bow loops to complete the desired look.

5 To attach a garland to a tablecloth or skirt, insert two corsage pins, crossing them in an X at each point of attachment. Weave the pins in and out of the fabric twice. If the garland is quite heavy, use four pins in sets of two. Insert a small drapery hook, upside down, into the fabric just above the middle of the X. Hang the garland on the hook.

Tip *Make the bows ahead of time and store them apart from the garland. Roll the ribbon tails and secure them with paper clips to keep them from being crushed.*

WOODLAND GARLAND

Berries, crab apples, and woody stems give this garland a more casual flavor. A garland with foliage, berries, and woody vines is twisted together with a garland of boxwood, eucalyptus, and ruscus. Then stems of crab apples are wired to the garland for a bountiful effect. The garland can be dressed up with ribbons and flowers or dressed down with wood string and small vine wreaths.

Elegant Reception Tower

This tiered floral display, placed on an entrance table or at the center of a buffet table, is sophisticated and elegant. Though it appears to be a complicated professional design, it is really quite easy to create. The tower has small arrangements at the top and base and a teardrop cascade bridal bouquet that slips into the short upright tube.

The Lomey system of clear plastic parts, which can be purchased separately or in kits, makes the designing fun. Special glue holds the pieces together. Be sure to follow the glue manufacturer's directions. The florals and materials listed below are for the entire display. Divided lists are included with the directions for each section of the design.

FLORALS

- *One 4-ft. (1.2 m) bead garland with 10 vines, with three 9" (23 cm) strands per vine*
- *One ivy bush with six branches of varied lengths*
- *Seven medium parchment roses*
- *Nine large parchment roses*
- *Four parchment hydrangea blossoms*
- *10 white and off-white open silk roses*

TOOLS AND MATERIALS

- *Lomey glue*
- *One clear Lomey saucer, 6" (15 cm) diameter*
- *One clear Lomey saucer, 11" (28 cm) diameter*
- *Three clear universal pieces*
- *One rim pad*
- *One clear tube, 15" (38 cm) tall*
- *One clear tube, 30" (76 cm) tall*
- *Two pedestal foams (foam cages)*
- *Two beaded wreath rings, 4" (10 cm) diameter*
- *Green floral tape, ½" (1.3 cm) wide*
- *Elegant bridal bouquet holder*
- *Wire cutter*
- *Glue pan and glue pillows*
- *3 cups decorative marbles or sea glass*

1 Read the directions on the Lomey glue tube. Apply glue to the ring on the underside of the small saucer. Glue it to the center underside of the large saucer. Set them on the work surface with the large saucer on top. Glue two universal pieces to the large saucer, halfway between the rim and center, at 1:30 and 10:30. (Place the tubes on the universal pieces to be sure they are perfectly parallel, but then remove the tubes to allow the glue to set.) Glue the rim pad onto the rim of the larger saucer at 6:00. Glue a foam cage to the rim pad. Glue another foam edge onto the third universal piece. Allow the glue to set.

2 Remove the three-strand vines from the beaded garland. Gently insert two bead streamers, one at a time, into the short clear tube. Insert four streamers, one at a time, into the long, clear tube.

3 Cut the ivy bush into pieces as follows: one stem 30" (76 cm) long, four stems 6" (15 cm) long, and the rest into small pieces with two to five leaves each.

4 Remove the floral tape holding the hydrangeas together. Gently remove the blossoms and divide each parchment hydrangea into five separate floret clusters. Wrap the small bunches together with floral tape, keeping the stems as long as possible.

5 Divide the florals into three groups as noted for the bridal bouquet, the top design, and the base design. Then work on each section of the design.

2

Bridal Bouquet

FLORALS

- *One ivy streamer, 6" (15 cm) long*
- *Several small ivy stems*
- *Two large parchment roses*
- *Four medium parchment roses*
- *Six silk roses*
- *One-third of the hydrangea clusters*
- *Beaded wreath ring*

1 Place the bouquet holder into the short clear tube. It will be a secure fit. Place the 4" (10 cm) beaded wreath ring around the base of the bouquet holder. You will be able to secure it in place as you insert stems.

2 Insert a 6" (15 cm) ivy stem into the front of the foam at 6:00, draping down with a gentle arch. Add small pieces of ivy around the base of the holder, inserting them so they hold the wreath in place.

3 Cut the stems of the large parchment roses 4" (10 cm) long. Insert one at 2:00 the other at 9:00.

4 Cut the stem of one silk rose 6" (15 cm) long; cut the others 4" (10 cm) long. Insert the long one into the lower right draping it down over the ivy streamer. Insert one short rose at 4:00, one at 2:30 under the parchment rose, one at 11:00, one on the top left of the foam, and the last one in the top center of the bouquet.

5 Cut the stem of one medium parchment rose 5" (12.7 cm) long. Insert it at 6:00, draping over the ivy. Cut the other three stems 4" (10 cm) long. Insert one 4" above and to the right of the longer stem. Insert the second and third short roses at 10:30, one above the other.

6 Insert the hydrangea blossoms in and around at random to cover mechanics and add texture. Add ivy stems where needed.

7 Work the beaded wreath ring strands up into the bouquet.

Top Design

1 Insert the loose universal piece with the foam cage into the long tube. Remove the plastic spines from three large ivy leaves. Hot-glue the leaves onto the bottom of the universal piece, with the right sides of the leaves facing down and out.

2 Gently place the beaded wreath ring over the top of the foam; rest it on the universal piece.

3 Place the long ivy strand into the top of the foam at 3:00, forming and draping it down around the clear tube. Place the last 6" (15 cm) garland on the opposite side, draping to the left. Intertwine two bead strands with the hanging ivy.

4 Cut the stems of four large parchment roses to 5" (12.7 cm). Insert them, one at a time, into the side of the foam, facing down a bit at 11:00, 1:00, and 4:00; insert the last one in the center.

5 Cut three silk roses with stems 4", 5", and 7" (10, 12.7, and 18 cm) long. Insert the short rose at 3:00. Insert the other two at 6:00, draping down over the ivy.

6 Insert the medium parchment rose into the top, facing the front of the design.

7 Insert the hydrangea blossoms in and around at random to cover mechanics and add texture. Add ivy stems where needed.

8 Bring the beads of the wreath ring up and into the design.

FLORALS

- Ivy streamer, 30" (76 cm) long
- One ivy streamer 6" (15 cm) long
- Several small ivy stems
- Four large parchment roses
- One medium parchment rose
- Three silk roses
- One-third of the hydrangea clusters
- Beaded wreath ring

4

6

Base Design

1 Insert two 6" (15 cm) ivy stems into the foam, one on the right and one on the left.

2 Cut three large parchment roses with 5" (12.7 cm) stems. Insert one into the lower right, one into the lower left, and one draping forward in front.

3 Cut the silk rose stem 4" (10 cm) long and insert it in back facing the center of the design. Add the medium parchment roses to the lower front and right.

4 Insert the hydrangea blossoms, ivy, and last two beaded stems in and around at random to cover mechanics and add texture.

5 Fill the base saucer with decorative marbles or sea glass at the reception.

FLORALS

- *Two ivy streamers, 6" (15 cm) long*
- *Several small ivy stems*
- *Three large parchment roses*
- *Two medium parchment roses*
- *One silk rose*
- *One-third of the hydrangea clusters*

Trio of Centerpieces

When you create reception center-pieces, vary the styles and shapes to make the room more interesting. In these three designs, the floral ingredients are the same but they are put together in three completely different ways. The colors, containers, and flowers tie the arrangements together, but the overall look is more exciting.

A centerpiece should be designed so people can enjoy it but still converse across the table. The profiles and formal lines of the low bowl and pedestal arrangement shown here make them perfect for guest tables. The vase design would also be a great accent on a buffet table or near the guest book. The list below is enough for one of the designs. Multiply the amounts by the number of centerpieces you need.

FLORALS

- Four stems larkspur
- Six stems calla lilies with foliage
- One stem poppy with two flowers and one bud
- One stem alstroemeria with five flowers
- Five stems gardenia with one bud each
- One parchment hydrangea divided into five pieces
- One stem camellia leaves with three branches

TOOLS AND MATERIALS

- Low glass bowl for first design
- Glass vase for second design
- 6" (15 cm) Lomey dish; 12" (30.5 cm) pedestal; Eiffel Tower vase for third design
- One package iridescent crystal fiber
- One-third block white Styrofoam
- Clear anchor tape
- Wire cutter
- Knife
- Glue pan and glue pillows
- Glue gun and glue sticks

Low Bowl

1 Fill the bowl with most of the crystal fiber, pressing it into the sides and around the top. Reserve a small handful. Make a well in the center for the Styrofoam, and secure it with clear anchor tape. Lightly mark diagonal lines with your knife across the top of the foam, dividing it into four equal squares: north, south, east, and west.

2 Cut the larkspur stems to extend 12", 10", 8", and 6" (30.5, 25.5, 20.5, and 15 cm) beyond the foam. Insert the 12" stem in the side of the east area, hanging over the bowl edge and almost touching the table. Insert the other stems, longest to shortest, each slightly above the others, alternating from left to right of the first stem.

3 Cut the calla stems to extend 12", 10", 8", two 6", and 4" (30.5, 25.5, 20.5, two 15, and 10 cm). Bend and shape the stems so the blossoms open upward and the tips bend toward the table. Insert the stems into the west area in similar arrangement to the larkspur.

4 Cut the poppy into two flowers and one bud, keeping the stems as long as possible. Insert the bud stem into the south (front) section, draping down over the bowl. Insert the longer flower stem above and slightly to the right of the bud; turn the flower head up to face the sun. Insert the shorter flower stem near the center of the foam to the left of the first flower, facing upward.

5 Cut the alstroemeria to extend 5" (12.7 cm) from the foam. Insert the stem into the north (back) section, facing outward.

6 Cut two gardenia stems to extend 10" (25.5 cm) from the foam; cut the others to extend 8", 6", and 4" (20.5, 15, and 10 cm). Insert the stems, one by one, near the center of the foam, with the flower heads pointing in various directions. Direct the longer stems outward and keep the flower of the shortest stem low in the center of the arrangement.

7 Cut the camellia foliage into six pieces and insert them around the outside of the bowl and in the center to cover the foam. Insert the five parts of the hydrangea in and around the design where there are open spaces.

8 Lace some of the remaining crystal fiber around the top of the design to cover the mechanics. Extend the look by laying some fiber on the table at the base of the container.

Vase

1 Place the crystal fiber in the vase, reserving a small handful. Cut the Styrofoam to fit into the neck of the vase; secure it with anchor tape.

2 Cut the camellia foliage into six pieces. Insert them into the foam, draping over the edge of the vase.

3 Leave the larkspur stems long. Insert them, one by one, into the center of the foam at various angles.

4 Cut the calla stems to extend 12", 10", two 8", and two 6" (30.5, 25.5, two 20.5, and two 15 cm) above the vase. Insert the two longest stems in the center, offsetting the larkspur stems. Insert the two 8" stems into opposite sides, draping them over the vase edge. Insert the two shortest stems into the other two sides, closer to the vase lip.

5 Cut the poppy into two flowers and one bud, keeping the stems as long as possible. Insert the bud high in the center. Insert one flower at the lower back and the other to the front left; turn them to face upward.

6 Cut two flowers from the alstroemeria cluster, leaving the main stem to extend 10" (25.5 cm). Insert the long stem upward in the back. Insert the separated flowers in the front, facing forward.

7 Cut the gardenia bud to extend 12" (30.5 cm) from the foam, and insert it in the center, slightly front and right. Cut two gardenias to extend 8" (20.5 cm); insert them below the bud with one facing out and the other facing right. Cut the last two stems to extend 6" and 8" (15 and 20.5 cm), and insert them at the back near the vase lip.

8 Insert the five hydrangea parts in and around the design where there are open spaces. Lace some of the crystal fiber around the top of the design to cover the mechanics. Extend the fiber onto the table, if desired.

Pedestal

1 Glue the 6" (15 cm) Lomey dish onto the 12" (30.5 cm) pedestal using the Lomey glue. Allow to dry. Insert the pedestal into the Eiffel Tower vase.

2 Fill the dish with crystal fiber, reserving a small handful. Drape fiber down over the sides all around, hanging at various lengths 4" to 12" (10 to 30.5 cm) below the rim. Center the Styrofoam in the dish, and secure with crisscrossed anchor tape.

3 Leave the larkspur stems long. Insert them into the center of the foam like an explosion of fireworks.

4 Cut the calla stems to extend these lengths from the foam: one 12" (30.5 cm), two 10" (25.5 cm), and three 8" (20.5 cm). Bend and shape the stems so the blossoms open upward and the tips bend toward the table. Insert the longest stem in the bottom left; insert a 10" stem above it to the right and an 8" stem above that to the left, all radiating from the same point. Insert the other 10" stem in the bottom right, with one 8" stem above it to the right and the last one above that to the left.

5 Cut the poppy into two flower stems to extend 10" and 8" (25.5 and 20.5 cm) from the foam and one bud to extend 14" (35.5 cm). Insert the bud, draping to the front. Insert the 10" stem above it and to the left and the 8" stem above that and to the right. Turn the flowers to face upward.

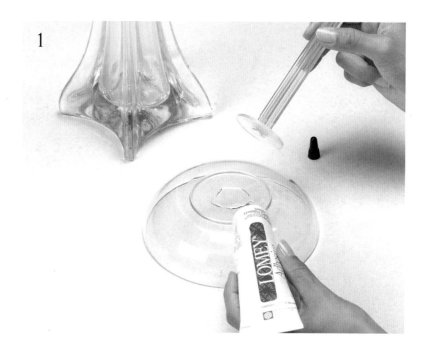

6 Cut two flowers from the alstroemeria cluster, leaving the main stem 8" (20.5 cm) long. Insert the stem in the back, facing slightly down. Insert the separated flowers in the front upper right.

7 Cut three gardenia stems to extend 10" (25.5 cm). Insert one high in the center, the second down over the right side, and the third between them and to the back. Cut the fourth stem to extend 8" (20.5 cm) and insert it deep into the same area. Cut the last stem short and insert it near the center to fill any empty space.

8 Cut the camellia foliage into six stems, leaving them as long as possible. Insert them hanging over the sides of the container. Insert the five hydrangea parts in any open spaces.

9 Lace the remaining crystal fiber over the design to cover the mechanics. Drape fiber down onto the table, if desired.

Place Cards and Table Markers

An assigned seating plan is a thoughtful way to include each guest in a circle of familiar faces and to mingle guests who may not know each other. Individual place cards and decorative table markers help guests find their special seats. Arranged above each place setting, they add a lot of color and charm to the reception room. They also become nice favors for guests. Look for miniature frames and vases at craft and floral outlets.

Mr. Joseph Schmidt

Ernest Olson

9

Miniature Vase

These mini vases have tiny heart-shaped glass feet that conveniently hold a place card. Dress them up with tiny bouquets and tie ribbons around their necks, trailing the tails alongside the place settings.

FLORALS

- *Bush of miniature roses and buds*
- *Bush of small ivy*

TOOLS AND MATERIALS

- *1 yd. (0.92 m) decorative ribbon, ⅝" (15 mm) wide*
- *Glue gun and glue sticks*
- *Floral tape*
- *Wire cutters*
- *Place card*

Nosegay

This simple-to-make place card favor uses miniature plants that can be selected to suit your wedding theme.

FLORALS

- *One miniature pansy plant or three pansy stems*

TOOLS AND MATERIALS

- *Small glass vase*
- *Glue gun and glue sticks*
- *24" (61 cm) 20-gauge decorative wire*
- *Wire cutter*
- *Pencil*
- *1 yd. (0.92 m) sheer ribbon, 1½" (39 mm) wide*
- *Scissors*
- *Place card*

Silver Frame

Small frames can be used to identify individual guests, and they make practical favors. Slightly larger frames can be used to number the tables.

FLORALS

- *Parchment hydrangea*

TOOLS AND MATERIALS

- *Place cards or table number cards*
- *Small silver frame*
- *Beaded wire stem*
- *Green floral tape*
- *Glue gun and glue sticks*
- *1 yd. (0.92 m) wired sheer ribbon, ⅞" (23 mm) wide*
- *Shears*
- *24-gauge wire, cut into thirds*

1 Tie the ribbon around the neck of the vase; make a two-loop bow.

2 Cut two rosebuds and four small leaves from the rose bush. Glue two leaves and a bud to the end of each ribbon tail.

3 Make a small bouquet of six to eight blossoms and buds and one ivy stem. Wrap the stems together just below the blossoms, using floral tape. Cut the stems 2½" (6.5 cm) long. Insert the bouquet into the vase and secure with a drop of hot glue inside the vase neck.

4 At the reception site, mount the place card on the holders and trail the ribbons on the table.

1 Cut the plant or flower stems to a length that allows the end of the stem to touch the bottom of the vase and the upper leaves to rest on the vase rim.

2 Remove three larger leaves from different places on the pansy plant or flowers. Remove the plastic veins. Wrap the leaf bases, overlapping, around the bottom of the plant stem; secure with touches of hot glue.

3 Place a dot of hot glue in the bottom of the vase, and insert the plant or flowers. Arrange the blossoms and buds.

4 Wrap one end of the decorative wire three times around a pencil; slip the loops off. Holding the loops just above the flowers, wind the rest of the wire down through the flowers and around the vase several times.

5 Tie the ribbon around the vase neck in a simple shoestring bow. Slip the place card between the wire loops above the flowers.

1 Print each place card or table number, and insert it in the frame.

2 Cut the beaded stem into four 12" (30.5 cm) pieces. Remove beads from the lower 4" (10 cm) of each piece.

3 Separate the hydrangea into small florets. Place one floret stem alongside the four beaded stems, 4" (10 cm) from the ends. Wrap the stems together with floral tape to the ends. Twist the stem ends around a pencil.

4 Glue the stems to the upper left of the frame.

5 Make a five-loop bow (page 24); tie it with the piece of wire and cut the wire short. Glue the bow under the flower.

Collection of Votive Favors

Collections of various votive favors that are related by color can be used as centerpieces on guest tables. Different floral materials are used for each favor; some have candles and some don't. The favors can be arranged in a cluster in the center of the table, perhaps on a mirror base to double their impact. As another option, the shorter favors can be placed above individual place settings, reserving the center of the table for a coordinating tall or low arrangement. Guests can be invited to take a favor when they depart. This is a good way to use up odds and ends of floral materials left over from the other wedding decorations while tying the guest favors to the wedding theme.

Beaded Taper

This favor, because of its height, should be placed near the center of the grouping. The wire and beads will not burn, but the flame should be extinguished before it reaches the crystal fiber.

TOOLS AND MATERIALS
- *Decorative votive holder*
- *White Styrofoam*
- *Knife*
- *Taper candle, 12" (30.5 cm) tall*
- *2½ yd. (2.3 m) beaded wire*
- *Glue gun and glue sticks*
- *Small amount of iridescent crystal fiber*

1 Cut a piece of Styrofoam to fit tightly in the votive, and glue it in place.

2 Using a knife, flatten one side of the candle, 1" (2.5 cm) from the bottom. Insert the taper securely into the Styrofoam. The flattened side keeps the candle from rotating.

3 Insert the beaded wire end into the foam and then wrap it several times around the outside of the votive in an irregular pattern. Continue wrapping to the top of the taper.

4 Place a small amount of iridescent crystal fiber into the votive to cover the foam.

Beaded Apple

Any elegant beaded fruit works well for this favor. You could also use a bird's nest, a bow, or a pinecone. If your wedding is near the holidays, use an ornament.

FLORALS
- *12 small rosebuds with foliage*
- *Seven leaves with short stems*
- *Beaded apple*

TOOLS AND MATERIALS
- *Decorative votive holder*
- *White Styrofoam*
- *Glue gun and glue sticks*
- *One wood pick, 6" (15 cm) long*
- *Wire cutter*

1 Cut a piece of Styrofoam to fit tightly in the votive, and glue it in place.

2 Arrange the leaves around the rim of the votive holder, overlapping them with bases near the center of the foam. Glue in place.

3 Insert the pointed end of the wood pick up into the bottom of the apple; glue in place. Cut off the wired end, leaving about 2" (5 cm) extending. Place a circle of hot glue on the top of the foam and leaves. Insert the wood pick into the foam and push down until the apple is secured to the foam.

4 Cut off the stems of the rosebuds. Glue the buds in a ring around the base of the apple.

Miniature Nosegay

Choose miniature nosegays to suit your style and color scheme.

FLORALS

- *Nosegay of miniature roses*

TOOLS AND MATERIALS

- *Decorative votive with votive candle*
- *18" (46 cm) decorative cording*
- *Floral tape*
- *Wire cutter*
- *Glue gun and glue sticks*

1 Tie a knot in each end of the decorative cording. Tie the cording around the votive in a simple bow.

2 Using floral tape, wrap the rose stems together just below the blossoms. Cut the rose stems to 1" (2.5 cm). Insert the stems under the cording so the bouquet rests above the bow. Secure with glue.

Pansies

Shape the pansy stems in dramatic curves and point their pretty faces toward the sun.

FLORALS

- *Two pansy flowers with foliage*
- *One stem lily of the valley*

TOOLS AND MATERIALS

- *Decorative votive holder*
- *White Styrofoam*
- *1½ yd. (1.4 m) raffia*
- *Wire cutter*
- *Glue gun and glue sticks*
- *Moss*

1 Cut a piece of Styrofoam to fit tightly in the votive, and glue it in place.

2 Cut the raffia into three equal lengths, and tie them together in a knot around the votive holder, ½" (1.3 cm) below the rim. Glue in place.

3 Cut the pansy stems 6" and 2" (15 and 5 cm) long. Insert the flowers and foliage into the foam.

4 Cover the foam with moss.

Orchid Blossoms

Elegant wire and rhinestone accents complement the lines of the ribbon and orchid bud stem.

FLORALS

- *Two dendrobium orchid blossoms and a stem with several small buds*

TOOLS AND MATERIALS

- *Decorative votive with votive candle*
- *18" (46 cm) wired satin ribbon, 1½" (39 mm) wide*
- *Shears*
- *Glue gun and glue sticks*
- *Three decorative wire accents*
- *Wire cutters*

1 Tie the ribbon in a loose square knot around the votive.

2 Glue the bud stem into the knot. Cut the blossoms from the stems, and glue them above the knot.

3 Cut the decorative accents to 3", 2", and 1" (7.5, 5, and 2.5 cm). Insert the two longer pieces into the lower right side of the knot, following the angle of the bud stem. Insert the short piece into the upper left side.

4 Bend and crinkle the ribbon.

Top the Cake

Flowers adorning the wedding cake tie it into the color theme of the wedding. When you use faux flowers instead of fresh, you avoid the risk of getting the frosting wet. A simple topper like this one, designed in a plastic base, might repeat flowers used in the bride's bouquet or in other arrangements around the reception site. The base keeps the floral materials from touching the cake—you should avoid inserting any flowers directly into the frosting. The design can be made ahead of time and set atop the cake at the reception. Small projections on the underside of the base keep the topper in place. Be sure to coordinate with the cake baker the size, shape, and colors of the floral topper.

FLORALS

- *Five small foam roses*
- *One stem lisianthus with two flowers and one bud*
- *One stem hydrangea*
- *One stem caspia*

TOOLS AND MATERIALS

- *Lace cake topper base*
- *⅙ block floral foam*
- *Knife*
- *Glue pan and glue pillows*
- *Wire cutter*
- *Two decorative wire accents*

1   Cut the foam to fit tightly into the cake topper base with the top 1" (2.5 cm) above the rim of the base. Dip the foam in the glue pan and secure it into the topper base.

2   Cut the two blossoms and one bud from the lisianthus, leaving 2" (5 cm) stems. Insert one blossom into the center top. Insert the second blossom into the top left. Insert the bud into the lower right.

3   Cut the rose stems to 2" (5 cm). Insert four roses, evenly spaced, around the lower edge of the holder. Insert the fifth rose between and to the right of the lisianthus blossoms.

4   Cut the hydrangea into separate florets, leaving 2" (5 cm) stems. Insert the stems into the foam so the blossoms fill in all the empty spaces.

5   Cut the caspia into 12 small pieces. Insert them into the design for color, texture, and depth.

6   Insert the wire accents off-center in the top of the design.

1

3

4

SUGARED ROSE

This simple, elegant cake topper is the perfect complement to your wedding cake if your flower of choice is the red rose. All you need is one long-stem open red rose, a 12" (30.5 cm) ivy vine, 12 iridescent white corsage leaves, and a Mini-Deco holder. This rose came "glazed" with faux sugar crystals. Cut the blossom and individual leaves from the rose stem. Insert the blossom into the top of the foam. Secure the ends of the ivy into the foam at the sides to form an arch. Form a collar with the rose leaves and add the white corsage leaves for accents. Tie a small bow to the ivy arch and let the ribbon ends cascade down around the cake.

Bride's Surprise Toss Bouquet

This is a clever toss bouquet made up of several small bundles of flowers. The stems of each floral bundle are wrapped with ribbon. Then all the bundles are arranged into a hand-tied bouquet, secured only with a contrasting bow. You can use any combinations of flowers, accent flowers, and foliage for the small bundles, so this is a good project to use up the materials left over from other wedding designs. Only the bride knows that when it is time to toss the bouquet, she will turn around, secretly untie the bow that holds the bouquet together, and toss the bundles over her shoulder. As the single women scurry to catch the bouquet, they will be surprised to find their chances have multiplied.

FLORALS

- *Variety of flowers and foliage to match the color scheme of the wedding*

TOOLS AND MATERIALS

- *Green anchor tape*
- *Double-face satin ribbon, 1½" (39 mm) wide; 12" (30.5 cm) for each bundle plus 1 yd. (0.92 m) for tying the bouquet*
- *Scissors*
- *Wire cutter*
- *Two colors of ¹⁄₁₆" (1.5 mm) ribbon, 18" (46 cm) per bundle*
- *Glue pan and glue pillows or glue gun and glue sticks*

1 Determine how many floral bundles you want. Separate the florals into groups of similar flowers and foliage. If some florals do not have stems, reserve them until the end.

2 Form a small bouquet, taking one or two flowers and foliage stems from each group. Wrap the stems together with anchor tape just below the lowest blossom and again a few inches down the stems. Repeat until you have made the desired number of bundles. Cut the stems so all the bundles are about the same length.

3 Cut a 12" (30.5 cm) length of wide ribbon. Touch one end of the ribbon in the glue, and fold it over the stem ends. Turn the ribbon and wrap the stems tightly to the top; secure at the top with glue. Angle-cut the end and leave a short tail. Repeat for each bundle.

4 Cut an 18" (46 cm) length of each color of narrow ribbon, and tie them in a knot or small bow at the top of the ribbon wrap.

5 Glue in any florals without stems, distributing them among the bundles.

6 Form the bundles into a hand-tied bouquet, as in steps 3 to 6 on page 44. Using 1 yd. (0.92 cm) of wide ribbon, tie the bundles together in a bow that can be easily untied. Keep it a secret!

4

Toasting Glasses for the Bride and Groom

Add an innovative, charming detail to the traditional champagne toast with floral rings that hug the glass stem bases. Make them just for the bride and groom, or make them for the entire head table for a colorful display as glasses are lifted in a toast to the new couple.

The materials list and instructions are for two floral rings. Each floral ring is a large composite rose, made from the individual petals of two open roses. To fit the wedding theme, you can choose another multi-petal flower, such as lily, dahlia, lisianthus, or anemone.

FLORALS

- Four long-stemmed large, open garden roses
- Six gold rose leaves, 2½" (6.5 cm) long

TOOLS AND MATERIALS

- Cardboard for two discs
- Newspaper
- Moss green spray paint
- Wire cutter

- ⅔ yd. (0.6 m) ivory and gold ribbon, 1½" (39 mm) wide
- Scissors
- Glue gun and glue sticks

1 Cut out two cardboard discs, each 4" (10 cm) in diameters. Then cut a 1" (2.5 cm) hole in the center of each disc. Cut a slit in each disc from the outer edge to the hole. Lay the discs on newspaper and spray paint both sides of the discs with the moss green paint.

2 Cut the individual rose leaves from each stem, and remove the plastic veins. Glue the rose leaves, wrong side down, overlapping around both sides of each disc. The leaf bases should be just a bit over the center hole and the leaf tips should extend beyond the outer edge. The leaves can overlap the slit but should not keep it from opening. Add three gold leaves to each disc, evenly spaced, on the top side.

3 Cut four 4" (10 cm) ribbon pieces; angle-cut one end of each. Glue two pieces to the top of each disc, overlapping the straight ends and spreading the tails slightly. Cut two more 4" pieces and bend each into a loop. Glue one loop over the left streamer on one disc and the other over the right streamer on the other disc.

4 Remove the calyxes (the green parts at the base of the flower) from the blossoms. Cut the individual petals from each layer and keep them in groups of large, medium, and small petals. Discard any plastic supports.

5 Touch hot glue to the inner cut edge of one large petal and secure it to the top of the leaf-covered disc near the inner circle. Repeat with a second petal, overlapping the first one slightly. Continue attaching petals, working in a spiral pattern from largest to smallest until the disc is covered. Allow the smaller petals to close up the center hole slightly, but keep the slit free.

3

5

6 Open the cut in the disc and slip the stem of the champagne glass into the center of the disc. Let the disc rest on the base of the glass. Fluff the petals up around the stem.

Index